NOV 26 '75   BAKER ST.

S0-AKY-498

A11703 644150

746.43   COP 2 ✓   SHELF LIST
                            AEI1086
WALLER, IRENE.
    TATTING: A CONTEMPORARY ART FORM.
IRENE WALLER. CHICAGO: H. REGNERY CO.,
1974.
    96 P.: ILL., 26 CM.

Tatting

a contemporary art form

Irene Waller

HENRY REGNERY COMPANY
CHICAGO

Copyright © 1974 by Irene Waller

All rights reserved. No part of this publication may be reproduced, stored
in a retrieval system, or transmitted, in any form or by any means,
electronic, mechanical, photocopying, recording, or otherwise, without the
prior written permission of the publisher.

First published in England in 1974 by Studio Vista

Published 1974 by Henry Regnery Company
114 West Illinois Street, Chicago, Illinois 60610

Library of Congress Catalog Card Number: 73-20930

ISBN: 0-8092-8394-8

Filmset and printed by
BAS Printers Limited, Wallop, Hampshire, England

Contents

Acknowledgements 6

Introduction 7

Abbreviations 8

Threads 9

1 Tatting history 11

2 Tatting characteristics 16

3 Technical terms 23

4 Working with one thread, the ring 27

5 Working with two threads, the line 41

6 Working with two threads, rings and lines together 47

7 Varying the approach 50

8 Finishing processes 53

9 Design sources and media 59

10 Organizing design 64

11 Completed objects, fabrics and design suggestions 71

Bibliography 91

Suppliers 93

Index 95

Acknowledgements

My thanks first to two people: Judy Roberts, who helped me in carrying out much of the practical tatting needed for the book, and Alan Hill, who took most of the photographs. I am greatly indebted to them both.

My thanks go also to those friends who helped me check the book, to those who contributed designs, to manufacturers and suppliers who assisted with information, and to Carole Sizer who typed the manuscript.

Credits

Photographs, except where otherwise stated, are by Alan Hill, Birmingham, England, the drawings and diagrams by the author. Tatting, except where otherwise stated, was designed and produced by Irene Waller or produced by Judy Roberts. Shoe bases supplied by Lotus and Bally. Evening shoes manufactured by Clarkes. Prototype large shuttle by Morrell.

Introduction

The pre-packaged character of life today divorces us from our roots and the essence of ourselves. This accounts for the tremendous revival of interest in the crafts as a means of self-expression and as a satisfying method of revitalizing our undernourished senses of sight and touch.

The purpose of this book is to consider tatting as a technique worthy of a contemporary revival and as a valid present-day art-form. It is intended to be read and worked through simultaneously.

Abbreviations

cr	close the ring
dk	double knot
l	line
lp	large picot
p	picot
r	ring
rep	repeat
sep	separated
tw	turn the work upside down
×4	four times

Threads

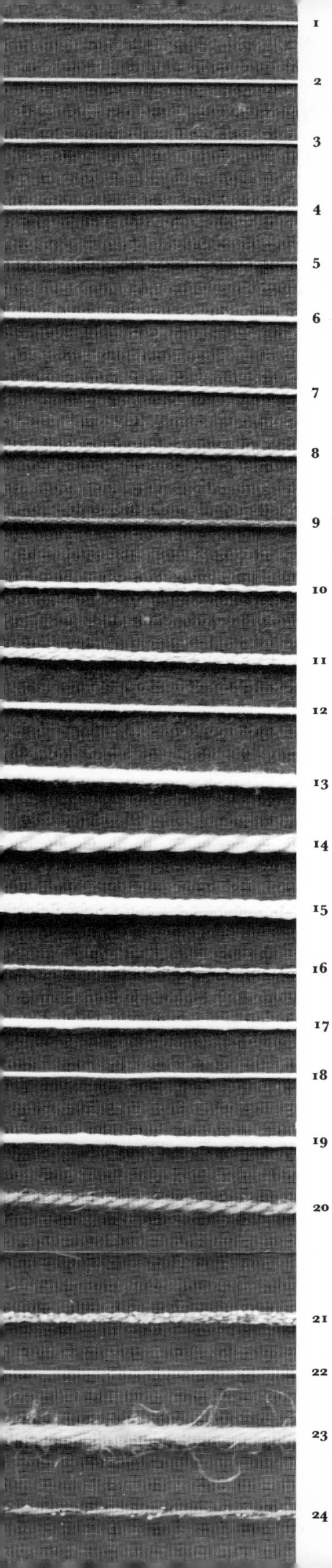

Fig. 1

1 'Sylko' no. 40, Dewhurst (UK)
2 Chain Mercer crochet no. 60, J. & P. Coats (UK)
3 Chain Mercer crochet no. 40, J. & P. Coats
4 Chain Mercer crochet no. 20, J. & P. Coats
5 'Twenty', Twilley (UK)
6 Cronita, Clark (UK)
7 D.M.C. Cotton Perlé, Dollfus Mieg & Co. (France)
8 'Lyscordet' (UK)
9 'Crysette', Twilley
10 'Goldfingering', Twilley
11 'Double Gold', Twilley
12 Lysbet, Twilley
13 Health Vest no. 1, Twilley
14 'Perlita', Clark
15 'Novacord', Atlas (UK)
16 Star-dust lamé non-tarnishable metallic, Jacmore Co., New York (USA)
17 Anchor Stranded, Clark
18 Silver Elastic Thread (USA)
19 Polypropylene string
20 'Penelope' Crewelwool
21 'Candlelight', made in France by Sildorex for 'Emu' Wools Ltd, Keighley (UK)
22 Metallic Cord, Wm Briggs & Co., Bromley Cross, Bolton (UK)
23 Jute Yarn
24 Composite yarn of two strands 2/12s weaving cotton and one of Hutchinson's 'Shimmerette'.

(NB: Crochet cottons have numbers – the higher the number the finer the thread.)

9

1   Tatting history

Fig. 3

Fig. 2
Looking-Glass Tree II Panel incorporating
appliqué, knotting and tatting. In cotton
fabric, net, wool yarn, 'Crysette', beads,
paillettes and mirrors. The tatting
forming the frame was stiffened with
P.V.A. solution. (Property of Dr & Mrs
Hayward, Warwick, England)

It is interesting to know something of the history of tatting. It did not, like the legendary Venus, spring entire from the waves, but developed slowly over the years, waxing and waning both in popularity and in the speed of its development, until it evolved into the form that we know today.

It obviously evolved from simple knotting, one of man's earliest textile techniques and of Eastern origin. In England and Europe during Medieval times, knotted thread, produced with the fingers or a needle, was used in vast quantities for outlining shapes in embroidery. The thread was knotted at frequent intervals to produce a bead-like formation which was then couched down with tiny stitches to outline patterns and shapes (fig. 3). But knotting reached its zenith in Europe in the seventeenth century, probably receiving a boost via the Dutch and their trading connections with the Chinese, who were using knotted threads extensively in their embroideries. Its uses were soon extended from the outlining of embroidered shapes to the production, with the aid of a shuttle, of more complex knotted edges and fringes for clothing, bed covers, bed curtains and the like (there is a beautiful knotted bed fringe in Sulgrave Manor, Oxfordshire, home of the ancestors of Washington). Its popularity was enormous and knotting became a favourite pastime particularly with the aristocracy, since it had a practical application, was easy to carry around and also showed off the hands to advantage, thus giving the knotter an air of both industry and grace. For this reason, knotting is often seen in the portraits of the period. Knotting bags and shuttles became valued objects, often given and received as presents, of great beauty and workmanship, created in ivory, tortoiseshell and precious metals, and embellished with jewels, enamelling or carving (fig. 4). Towards the end of the eighteenth century the passion for knotting declined and

11

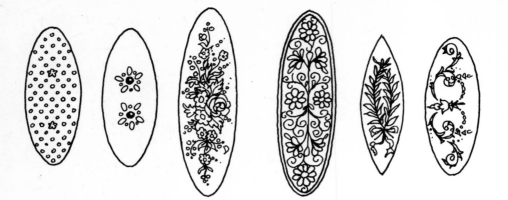

these beautiful shuttles began to be collectors' items. At the same time, however, there are indications, gleaned from diaries and account books, with their references to the existence of pairs of small shuttles, that a form of true tatting was now being practised.

Tatting, as such, is said to have originated in Italy in the sixteenth century. Simple rings were produced in rows or allowed to form rosette-like shapes and these very small pieces of work were then either tied or sewn together to form larger pieces. How this form of textile construction travelled from Italy further west does not seem to be very clear but travel it did, because by 1800 English literary references indicate that tatting had become a popular occupation.

The art of tatting may then have declined because the first book we have which gives instructions for it, *The Ladies Handbook of Millinery, Dressmaking and Tatting*, published in 1843, states, 'This kind of ornament . . . was once in high repute and again appears likely to become a favourite.' This it certainly did because in 1850 Mlle Eleanore Riego de la Branchardière, a prolific and creative needlewoman and author, who lived in London, brought out the first of her eleven publications on tatting. In the eighteen years covered by the production of these writings she transformed the craft. Until then it had been little more than the production of rings, with picots (the small decorative loops) as ornament, using one thread. The rings were left in rows or formed into rosettes, the resulting small fragments being laboriously sewn or tied together. Mlle Riego discovered how to use picots to join either ring to ring thus stabilizing the work, or motif to motif, or one row or round of rings to another thus enabling larger pieces of work to be produced. She also invented the use of a central ring with picots as a firm centre for a motif. However, for these things she used a needle, not a shuttle, as no one had yet worked out how to join by means of the picot while the thread,

Fig. 4 (r. to l.)
Knotting shuttle: silver on tortoiseshell
Tatting shuttle: Tunbridge ware
Knotting shuttle: pierced steel
Knotting shuttle: silver and gold on
tortoiseshell
Tatting shuttle: mother of pearl
Knotting shuttle: gold on tortoiseshell

Fig. 5

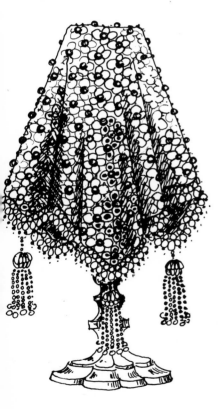

Fig. 6
Chalice veil by Queen Marie of Romania (*c.* 1900). Rich regular tatting encrusted with pearls and embellished with beaded tassels.

wound on a shuttle, had no free end. Fortunately, in 1851 an unknown writer solved this problem and published instructions on how to do it.

With these discoveries three big problems were solved which freed the technique for much greater creativity, (a) the elimination of tying or sewing motif to motif and ring to ring, (b) having enough continuous thread wound on the shuttle to produce a fairly big piece of work before a new thread became necessary, and (c) the resulting greater durability of the work in wearing and washing due to secure joins and the absence of tying points.

During the Riego period Mrs Beeton included in her *Book of Needlework* (1870) a section on tatting using Riego's improvements. There is also a largish section on tatting in the *Dictionary of Needlework* by Caulfeild and Saward which was published in 1882.

The next revivalist was Mlle Thérèse de Dillmont, of Alsace, who included a chapter on tatting in her *Encyclopaedia of Needlework*, published in 1886. (This book, still available and still much in demand, has sold, at the last count, 1,590,000 copies.) She built on already known structures, combined tatting with crochet, originated the Josephine ring, and described how to use two colours.

After this, tatting yet again fell on dismal times until, in 1910, Lady Hoare wrote *The Art of Tatting*, illustrated with her own work and that of Queen Marie of Romania, an accomplished artist in the technique. Queen Marie made some exceedingly beautiful and creative pieces, often for the church or for her friends, incorporating gold threads and precious stones. Her work is really of surpassing beauty and it is well worthwhile trying to track down a copy of the book in order to study it. The objects and fabrics become rich jewelled textures which really add a new dimension to one's conception of the art (fig. 6).

13

Lady Hoare writes that 'With two shuttles and an inventive brain there is no end to the designs that may be invented', and it was she more than anyone who freed the technique from the tyranny of 'circles and adaptations of circles' using the line ('chain' or 'bar') and spaces of unworked thread as design forces in themselves rather than merely to link one ring to another. She indulged in quite free, delicate, floral forms, often appliquéd on to net (fig. 7). Finally, in 1924 Mlle Alice Morawska, a pupil of de Dillmont's, published *La Frivolité*, a book of designs based on and amplifying her teacher's work.

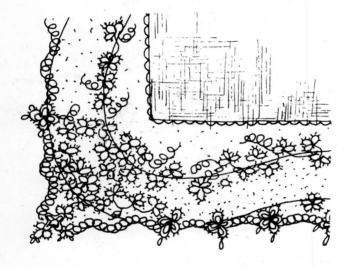

Fig. 7
Part of a piece by Lady Hoare. Net is appliquéd on to net, and the whole edging attached to cambric.

These authors, Riego, de Dillmont, Hoare and Morawska, not forgetting the unknown writer who so modestly and unassumingly gave the answer to the joining problem, developed and perfected the technique almost to its present state. While it is fair to assume that simultaneously other workers in other countries were wrestling with and solving technique and design problems, it is these ladies who put pen to paper for all to benefit.

Turning to the present day, Elgiva Nicholls has produced two books which have added considerably to the progression of tatting as an art form. *A New Look in Tatting*, published in 1959, suggests that tatting may be used in a very free, un-

14

trammelled manner and releases it still further from the tradition of repeating goemetric formations (fig. 8). The designs in the book fully display the line, unworked thread and picots, the latter sometimes cut and frayed, as important design factors. Her second book, *Tatting*, published in 1962, takes a sound and academic look at the subject as a whole.

Tatting, whether pieces of it or historical references to it, is not easy to track down. Often it has been removed from costumes for separate display and therefore it may be found in both costume and textile departments of museums. In the Victoria and Albert Museum, London, there are a few pieces in both departments and also a fair selection of books in the library. Tatting and knotting shuttles can sometimes be found in museums in the section devoted to needlework tools and occasionally old shuttles can be found in antique shops.

There are various portraits of ladies knotting and tatting: Joshua Reynold's portrait of the Countess of Albermarle (1759) is in the National Gallery, London, Allan Ramsay painted the Countess Temple (1766), Louis le Tocqué's Madame Danger is in the Louvre, and Nattier's Marie Adelaide de France is in the Musée de Versailles.

Fig. 8
Cow Parsley Freestyle tatting (c. 1962) by Elgiva Nicholls, using free-moving lines, large picots, cut picots and rings. The heads are three-dimensional in quality and the dragonfly wings enormous picots filled with cellophane.

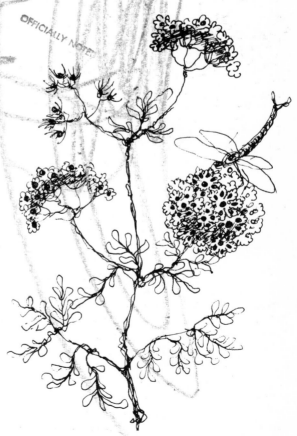

2   Tatting characteristics

Tatting is a knotted fabric structure which is open, firm and decorative. It is produced with thread by means of one or two small shuttles and the fingers. The visual elements which often predominate are basically rings or ovals and curved lines or semi-circles. These are formed of knotting and put together in innumerable different formations to form repeating patterns or freer, decorative shapes. The instant overall impression can be one solely of rings since the curves and semi-circles, when taking their part in the whole, often seem to become yet more rings. The work is open and light but also firm, and texturally the rings and curves have a clean, crisp, encrusted quality, derived from the character of the knotting itself, a running-line covered with tatting 'double knots'.

A conjectural derivation of the English word 'tatting' is that the work in its original form could only be made in very small pieces and these were considered to resemble a beggar's rags and tatters. *Tatters* itself is of Scandinavian origin, cf. Old Norse *taturr* and the Icelandic *töturr* – rags.

The names for tatting in other languages are fascinating. The German *Schiffchenarbeit*, meaning 'work of the little boat', is very descriptive of the appearance and movements of the shuttle. Italian *occhi*, meaning 'eyes', is equally descriptive but this time of the visual appearance. Finnish *sukkulapitsi* combines two words, *sukkula* (shuttle) and *pitsi* (lace). A second Finnish word for tatting, *karriko*, meaning 'a reef of rocks', describes the encrusted look of tatting. The Oriental name, *makouk*, indicates the shuttle. French *frivolité* and the Swedish derivative *frivolitet* are the only abstract names for tatting, although they are said to describe its character. The term *frivolité* has come to be used almost universally, certainly in Europe.

Neither the word '*tatting*' nor '*frivolité*' conjure up for me the nature and appearance of the work, the connotations of *tatting* being too dreary and *frivolité* too vague. I find *occhi* and *karriko* very descriptive and acceptable. *Sukkulapitsi* is a lovely beguiling word but, like 'a kind of lace', 'poor man's lace' and 'lace-making', misleading because true lace uses the twist as an element within it, whereas tatting does not.

The characteristics of tatting, visual and tactile, develop as a direct result of its natural components. The principal, unassailable element in tatting, there from its very beginning, is the tatting knot, recognizable as the lark's head or cow hitch knot (fig. 9). This is often called the 'tatting stitch' or 'double stitch' but, in fact, is a knot, not a stitch.

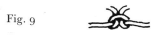

Fig. 9

The knots are carried side by side on an internal thread called a running-line (fig. 10). Because of their construction they produce more bulk on one side of the running-line than the other and the line therefore takes on a natural curve, which immediately determines the main characteristic of the work, its *curves* (fig. 11). A series of tatting knots on the running-line will not make a straight line willingly and, although a straight line can be manipulated, to do this to any extent is to use tatting in a manner foreign to it. The result is a sloppy handle, for in producing a straight line the knots cannot lie snugly side by side and at a slight angle to each other as they should naturally.

Fig. 10

Fig. 11

The simplest, earliest and oldest form of tatting is worked with one thread only. The thread is wound upon a small shuttle and the free end of the thread formed into a large loop over the fingers of the left hand and held between first finger and thumb. The right hand holds the shuttle and performs the motions over the loop necessary for the creation of the double knot. More precise instructions are given in chapter 4, but suffice it to say at this stage that the loop over the left hand is the portion of thread which makes the final visible knot itself, lying on a running-line of thread which comes from the shuttle in the right hand. (Remember that a running-line can move and slide inside the knots which cover it.) As the number of knots lying on the running-line increase so the loop on the left hand will become smaller as it is used up to make more knots. To make yet more knots the loop must be enlarged by being eased out so that knotting can continue. When a sufficient number of knots have been formed only one further thing can happen: instead of being eased out yet again to make further knots, the loop can instead be completely closed by pulling on the shuttle thread, and the result is a ring of knots, firm, neat, and with a very clean and firm outer edge formed by the 'heads' of the knots (fig. 12). Here we have encountered the second most important characteristic of the work and the reason for the Italian name *occhi* (eyes).

Fig. 12

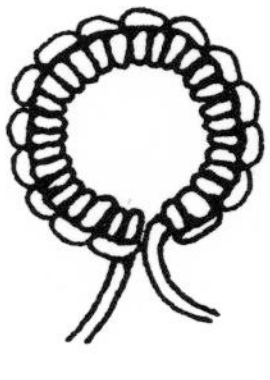

After another ring of knots is produced next to the first and is followed by a third, fourth and fifth ring, the work naturally takes on a geometric shape, which is characteristic number three (fig. 13). If many shapes are formed they can then be placed in juxtaposition to each other and held together in some way, thus beginning to form strips of fabric or areas of fabric (fig. 14). By far the most familiar, the most usual and easiest formations have this geometric quality. Rings produced a little distance away from each other with unworked thread in between will make lines of rings which naturally form simple edgings (fig. 15).

Fig. 13

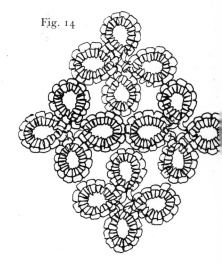

Fig. 14

In traditionally produced work, the curved lines and semicircles referred to on page 16 often add little more, except in a technical sense, to the visual and tactile characteristics of tatting as we generally know it, since they are composed of the same knots, and are often used merely to create further rings and curves. However, they are in fact a design force all of their own and, when used as such, are capable of much creative exploitation (fig. 16). The name for them has varied a great deal. Old ones include 'festoon' or 'feston', and the oldest of all is 'the straight thread'. Modern terms are 'chains', which suggests something akin to crochet, and 'bars', which sounds more like the straight bars produced in lace. Various other names suggested themselves, such as 'semicircles', 'semicircular bars', 'curves', 'curved bars' and 'links', but 'line' was chosen in the end as describing this element reasonably truthfully, and is therefore used in this book.

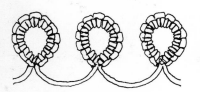

Fig. 15

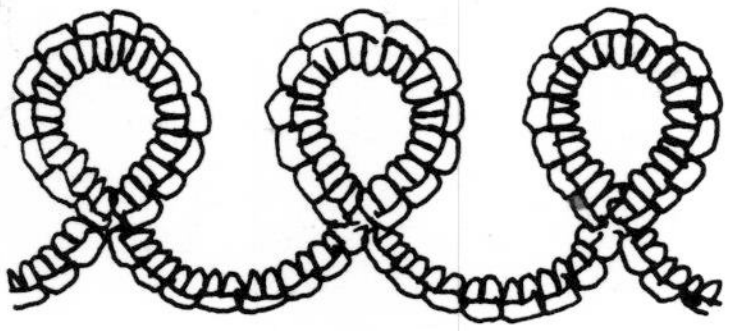

Fig. 16

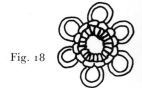

Fig. 17

The next element which adds something considerable is the picot (old names include 'pearl' or 'purl' and 'pearl loop'). Picots are small or large loops of thread between the double knots which, when produced, sit on the outer edge of all curves, i.e. the line of the heads of the double knots (fig. 17). They have two distinct functions, (a) decorative (fig. 18), and (b) to join ring to ring, ring to line, line to line, or motif to motif (fig. 19). Their decorative function, which, as we have seen, historically preceded their function as joining agents by many years, can alter the effect of tatting greatly; in general they give an added sense of decoration and airiness and lightness, but their exact placing and size can alter a basic fabric completely (figs. 20 and 21).

Fig. 18

Fig. 19

Fig. 20

Fig. 21
Six fabrics composed of the same motif but completely altered merely by the size and placing of the picots.

As joining agents they affect the technical aspect of the work very basically. We have considered the tatting double knot, then the ring of knots, then five rings of knots forming a pentagon-shape, or rings of knots with unworked thread in between forming a line of rings. A series of rings or ovals, by the very nature of their shape, will flop around in an un-manageable fashion; joining them together at a chosen point by means of the picot immediately gives the work stability. Joining motif to motif by means of the picot ensures that the work is securely and irrevocably joined.

The final characteristic is the natural manner in which basic shapes can be gradually and naturally elaborated into larger shapes such as circles, squares, hexagons etc. (fig. 22) or built up into strips of fabric, fabric yardage or shaped pieces (fig. 23).

Fig. 22

Fig. 23

We have been considering the basic components which go to form the whole and thus characterize the work. It must be stressed, however, that these were described purely as an aid to a visual and tactile appreciation of tatting in general, before one has seen or held an actual piece. *If tatting is to be a valid art-form today these basics must be used in a creative manner.* It is a technique unique in its qualities, and eminently capable of producing certain elements in the textile constructor's vocabulary. A technique should always reflect the skills and

Fig. 24
Venus Weaving by Tadek Beutlich,
Sussex, England.

requirements both aesthetic and practical of the day. Weaving, embroidery, knitting, macramé, knotting and many other constructions are all being used by artists and designers to express abstract concepts (fig. 24), as well as being used in a practical manner. There is no reason why tatting should not, like these other techniques, become a creative force in its own right.

Being composed basically of the one knot, tatting is an extremely easy technique to learn, the key lying almost solely in the mastery of this one knot, after which endless design variation is possible without further appreciable complication.

The only equipment required is a shuttle, suitable thread and dexterous, flexible fingers. Tatting *can* be produced with just the fingers, or a needle, but rhythm of movement and speed are both essentials of the technique and these can only be achieved properly by having the thread carefully wound on a well-shaped shuttle suitable to the individual's taste and needs, resting comfortably between the finger and thumb. It is perhaps the easiest of all forms of textile construction (those needing any equipment at all) to carry around.

Tatting is firm, strong and hard-wearing when properly produced. There is a face and a back to the work, although it has to be looked at very closely to be seen, particularly in fine work. The face is that on which the 'heads' of the knots lie in uninterrupted rows, while on the back they are interrupted where a picot occurs. This 'face' and 'back' element only becomes irritating when very heavy threads are used and even then it can be eliminated, if necessary, by quite simple means.

It should be added here that tatting can become visually displeasing if its natural shapes are distorted beyond their capacity.

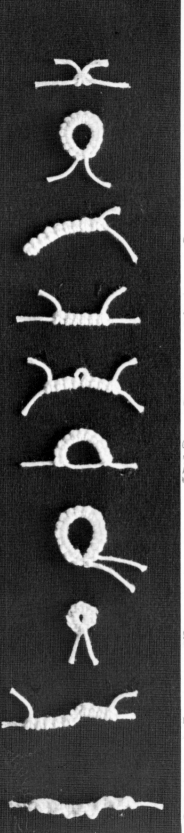

a
DS

b
Ring

c
curved chain

d
straight chain

e
picot chain

f
chain
½ ring
or
mock ring

g

h
small ring

i
locking stitch

j
chain
chain in
josephine knot
or knot stitch

Fig. 25

3 Technical terms

An illustrated list of tatting terms
used in the book.*

Tatting: A specialized form of knotted open work in which a
series of knots (fig. 25*a*) cover an internal core of thread.
Lengths of the resulting knotting are formed into either rings
(*b*) or lines, curved and straight (*c* and *d*), which then go
together to form the basic structure of the graphic whole.

Double knot: The complete tatting knot, composed of two
parts, a half hitch and a reversed half hitch. This is more
often called the tatting 'double stitch' but it is in fact a knot,
not a stitch. (*a*)

Ring: A loop of thread entirely covered with double knots
and drawn up tightly to form a firm ring or oval, sometimes
embellished with picots. Old names for the ring were loop,
lozenge, oval and rosette (*b*) and a small ring was a dot or
oillet.

Line: The term used *in this book* for a second and independent
thread covered with double knots, i.e. a thread that does not
have to be drawn up into a ring but can instead travel from
one point to another in the work. Other names were the
straight thread, festoon, chain or bar. (*c* and *d*)

Running-line: The core-thread of either ring or line on which
the double knots are carried.

Picot: A loop of thread formed between two double knots on
the outer edge of rings and lines. Picots can be of varying

*The instructional photographs accompanying chapters 3, 4, 5 and 6 are
all exact size. The samples were worked, for the most part, in Twilley's
'Crysette'. All threads referred to in the text by numbers are illustrated in
fig. 1 on page 9.

sizes and are used for two purposes, either pure ornament or as a means of joining ring to ring, line to line, ring to line or motif to motif (*e*).

Half-ring: A ring not totally drawn up, leaving a portion of thread unworked (*f*).

Mock-ring: The shape made when the line takes a form resembling a ring (*g*).

Josephine-ring: A ring, generally small, made of a series of half-knots (either half) only. Other names are Josephine knot, Josephine picot, or Josephine rosette (*h*).

Locking stitch: The name for a single knot or half-knot which is not 'turned', thereby deliberately locking the passage of the running-line (*i*).

Node stitch: Three half-hitches and three reversed half-hitches or the like (instead of one and one) making a braid with nodule-like formations. Can be used for rings or lines (*j*).

Josephine line: A line of half-hitches or of reversed half-hitches only.

Unworked thread: Occurs when working with one thread and is a portion of thread left without a covering of double knots (as in fig. 25*f*).

Unturned double knot: Occurs when working with two threads. The working shuttle thread is allowed to knot over the left-hand thread, the knot remaining unturned. It is used when tatting in heavy threads to eliminate the 'backs' of picots appearing on the face of the work.

Rows: Successive additions of further tatting in straight work.

Rounds: Successive additions of further tatting in circular work.

Triangle, Square, Pentagon, Hexagon etc: Shapes formed by three, four, five, six or more rings (fig. 26).

24

Fig. 26

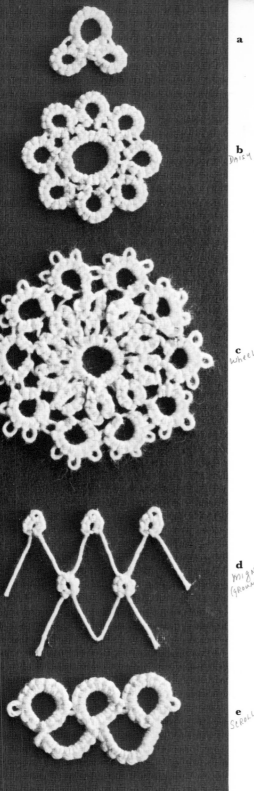

Tatting terms which describe traditional motifs are listed here (fig. 27) but except for 'scroll' are rarely referred to later in the book as they seem loaded with design implication.

Clover : A group of three rings, joined together, the centre ring larger than the others (*a*).

Daisy : A central picot-bearing ring carrying around it about eight rings, joined together (*b*).

Wheel : A central picot-bearing ring on to which is added another round of rings standing on either side of a line. Every second ring is attached to the picot of the central ring (*c*).

Mignonette stitch : One name given to the technique of leaving long spaces of unworked thread between rings. Caulfeild & Saward call it 'tatting ground work' (*d*).

Scroll : A series of rings connected by curved lines (*e*).

Medallion : Any complex motif, usually circular or square, which is a complete design in itself and resembles a medallion.

Scallop : An edging of any construction resembling scallop shells.

Fig. 27

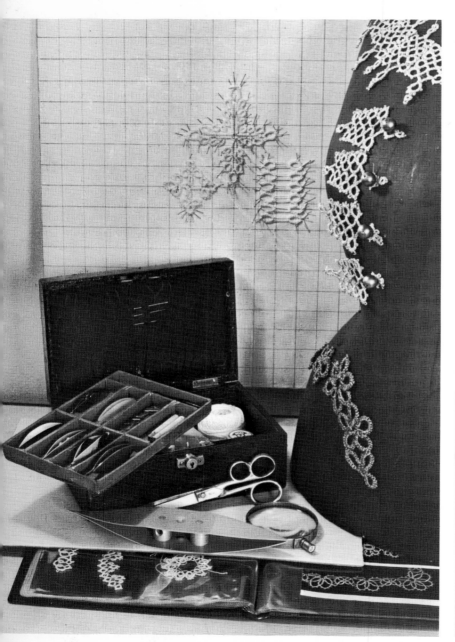

Fig. 28
1 Blocking-board of 'Celotex' covered with a sheet of squared paper and clear plastic sheet. The washed tatting is pinned out and left to dry to set in its correct shape.
2 Dressmaker's stand on which to design. (This one is an antique; a contemporary shape is obviously more useful.)
3 Tatting box to take work, threads, tatting instructions and large scissors in the base, shuttles, hooks and small scissors in the tray and needles and pins in the lid. (This one is an old Victorian trinket box.)
4 Sketchblock
5 Monster shuttle
6 Magnifying glass
7 Notebook with samples

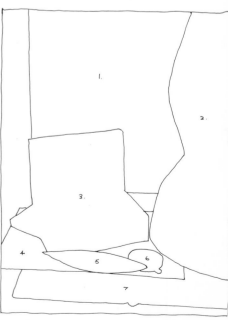

4 Working with one thread, the ring

It would be easy to give simple instructions for tatting together with apparently quite complex 'patterns' for objects and fabric, thus making it seem that one can accomplish advanced work very quickly. Here, however, the instructions are set out to take the worker gradually through a series of examples exploring each stage fairly comprehensively before carrying on to the next. The result should be twofold – a complete understanding of the process, plus a realization that creative and *individual* concepts are possible right from the beginning.

Equipment

To commence practical work, first choose a suitable thread (see fig. 1). It should be a firmly twisted, lustrous, non-hairy yarn. Crochet yarns of various thicknesses are the ones generally used for normal tatting (nos. 20, 40 and 60).

The next step is to choose a shuttle, and if the shuttle has no point or hook on it you will also need a fine crochet hook. There are various types of shuttle to choose from and it is a good idea to collect them so that you can decide for yourself which is the easiest to use. In fig. 28 the following are seen in the tray, starting from the left and working down (see also fig. 29*a–f*).

a Milward's (UK)   Light and good to hold as the finger and thumb sit in depressions in the blades. Very flexible yet grips yarn firmly. Will take quite heavy yarn. Has no hook.

b Morrell's Aero (UK)   Light, good to hold, does not slip out of the fingers. The point obviates the use of crochet hook. Yarn control by the blades very firm therefore will not take heavy yarn. Hole in the centre block for fastening on yarn.

Fig. 29

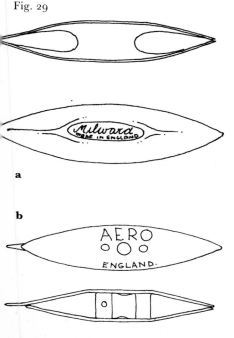

a

b

27

c Morrell's New Aero (UK) Light, good to hold, does not slip out of fingers, the hook on the end being better than the point for pulling through yarn. Separate bobbin for yarn which only unwinds when pulled. Extra bobbin. Projection on end of shuttle on which to place bobbin for winding.

d Boye's (USA) Light. Point for pulling thread through. Hole in centre block for fastening thread on.

OFFICIALLY NOTED

e Susan Bates' (USA) Separate bobbin for yarn. Hook on end for pulling thread through.

f Unknown A small, light plastic shuttle with a hole in centre block. Very pleasant to use in spite of lack of point or hook.

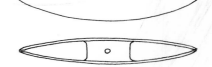

g Morrell's Monster Shuttle This was made especially for experimental work by Morrell but is a prototype. There are none on the market. One loses the rhythm of tatting when forced to use a larger implement for heavy yarn. The only other solutions when working with very heavy thread are the fingers by themselves or a small netting needle. (5 in fig. 28)

Fig. 30

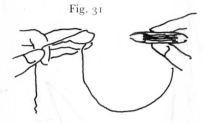
Fig. 31

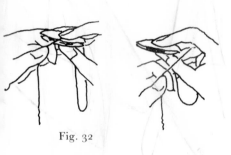

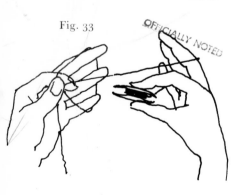
Fig. 32

Fig. 33

The tatting technique

Preliminaries

Wind the yarn on to the chosen shuttle carefully and evenly until the shuttle is full, i.e. until the yarn reaches but does not protrude beyond the edges of the blades or the edge of the bobbin. Cut off the yarn, leaving a free length of about 15 inches (38 cm.).

Hold the shuttle in the right hand between the finger and thumb with the thread coming from the back (fig. 30). Before proceeding any further practise this: take the free end of the thread in the left thumb and forefinger and then stretch it taut over the fingers of the left hand, winding it round the third finger if it will not stay taut (fig. 31). Now pass the shuttle right *under* the taut thread (fig. 32) and back *over*, then right *over* the taut thread and back *under*, allowing the taut thread to slip between either the finger and the shuttle or the thumb and the shuttle. You will find that a light but firm hold is necessary. Practise until you can do it quickly and without dropping the shuttle.

Making the double knot

With about 15 inches (38 cm.) of thread hanging free, hold the shuttle in the right hand between the finger and thumb with the thread coming from the back, as before. Take the free end of the thread between the thumb and forefinger of the left hand. Make a large loop around the outstretched fingers of the left hand, back to between the thumb and forefinger, and hold, slipping the second, third and fourth fingers of the right hand over and under the shuttle thread (fig. 33). Pass the shuttle under the loop of yarn (fig. 34) and then back over it (fig. 35). Then pull on the shuttle thread, very hard,

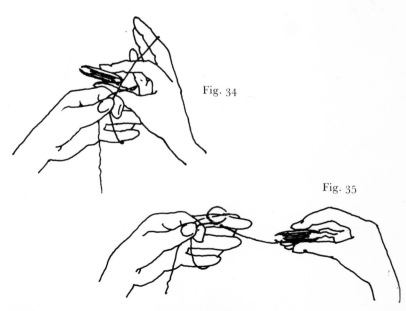
Fig. 34

Fig. 35

OFFICIALLY NOTED

using the fingers of the right hand as tensioners on the shuttle thread, and contract the fingers of the left hand, thus slackening the tension on the loop, so that the half-knot, *the formation of which has been created by the shuttle thread* (fig. 36) *becomes a knot made by the loop thread* (fig. 37). *This transfer of the knot is the whole core of the matter.* The movements of the tatting knot are created by the shuttle thread in the right hand, but by means of an interacting movement between the two hands (i.e. the hard pull on the shuttle thread, and the relaxing of tension on the loop thread), the loop thread on the left hand takes over as the knot and the knot which was *made* by the shuttle becomes a knot finally *formed* by the loop thread. You have made the first half of the double knot. To make the second half, with the shuttle between the first finger and thumb of the right hand but, this time, with the second, third and fourth fingers held out of the way, pass the shuttle *over* the loop of yarn and back *under* it and, as before, *pull*, with the fingers of the right hand acting as tensioners on the thread, so that, again, *the knot made by the shuttle thread becomes a knot formed by the loop thread.* You have now completed the tatting double knot (fig. 38).

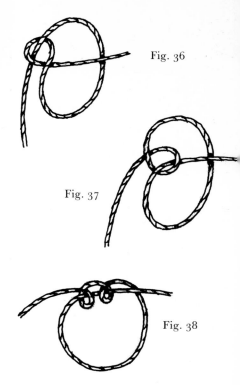

Fig. 36

Fig. 37

Fig. 38

Rings

Produce several double knots until the loop of yarn over the left hand is too small to allow the making of any more knots. Holding the line of knots between the thumb and fingers of the left hand, pull on the loop thread from below and make the loop larger. Continue knotting until sixteen knots have been completed. Holding the line of knots between the thumb and fingers of the left hand again, pull on the shuttle thread, drawing it back through the knots, and close the ring firmly. It is very important in tatting always to draw up the work tightly and firmly, not so tightly that it feels hard and begins to twist but sufficiently tightly to prevent any sloppiness or movement – one never sees the running-line showing through the knots. Tatting is essentially firm and stable but beginners tend to leave the work a little too loose in order to get on quickly.

Now fasten off. Fastening off, when necessary, is usually done by taking the ends of the threads to the back of the work and either sewing each one down separately with fine sewing cotton or threading on a needle (first one, then the other) and drawing each separately through the backs of the knots (see also chapter 8). However, purely for the purpose of these exercises, it is swifter to hold the ends down at the back with two very tiny dabs of fabric glue, such as 'Copydex'. Make sure your fingers are free of glue before continuing.

Fig. 40
Objects derived from rings only:
a Isolated rings attached to the main
hanging by nylon thread, and larger
rings hanging from their own long
threads. Areas of isolated rings together
with shapes made of rings. The thread
for this would have to be very heavy and
drape well.
b Bracelet of ring clusters in elasticized
metallic thread.
c Necklace and earrings of ring clusters
in metallic thread. The beads on fine
wire should add movement.
d Hanging of rings left attached to their
own thread. It looks and hangs well in
heavy white cords, the tatting being
done with the fingers.

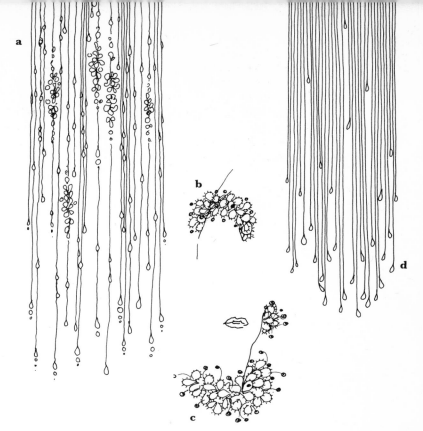

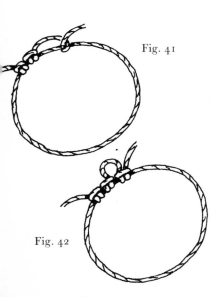

Fig. 41

Fig. 42

You have now made the ring (*a*) in fig. 39. When you have
practised making the larger ring of twenty-four knots (*b*), you
are ready to produce the items illustrated in fig. 40. (To link
rings together slip the previous ring on to the loop of thread
forming the new ring.)

Now produce a ring of twelve half-knots (*c*) only (it does not
matter which half as long as they are all the same). This is a
Josephine ring invented by de Dillmont at the time of the
Empress.

Making picots

Make two double knots on a ring. Make the first half of the
next double knot but leave it some distance away from the last
knot (fig. 41), make the second half and push the completed
knot close up to the previous one (fig. 42). You now have a
picot which can either be simply decorative (and in varying
sizes) or can have a joining function. In future, when counting
stitches or reading instructions, remember that the picot stands
between double knots but, in order to form it at all, the next

31

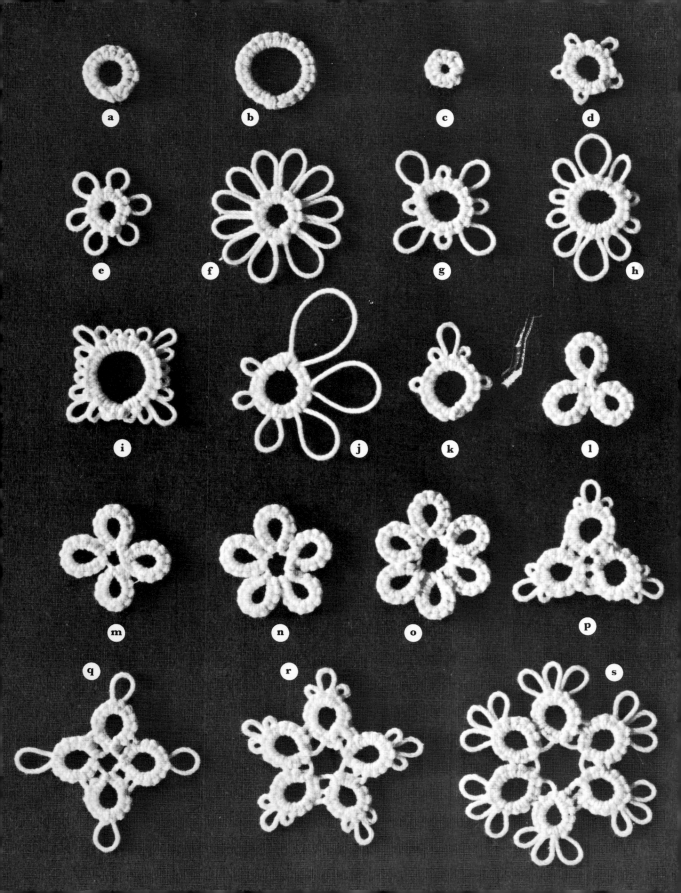

Fig. 39
Tatting with one thread.

double knot has to be made so that if an instruction reads 'make two double knots, make one picot, make one double knot' remember that you have already made the 'one double knot' by the very action of forming the picot. Continue the ring by making two more double knots, then make (one picot, three double knots) three times, and one picot one double knot. Close the ring and finish off (d).

The picot as ornament

Make a ring of twelve double knots with a largish picot between each two (e). If you find it difficult making large picots all the same size use something as a measure. Now make a ring of twelve double knots with larger picots between each double knot (f). Turn any of these last three rings over and look at the 'back' as opposed to the 'face' of the work. You will see that where picots occur there is a break in the heads of the knots. If the work is fine this is not noticed but in coarse work the break is unpleasant and the way of avoiding it is the unturned double knot described on page 42.

Now make a ring of sixteen double knots, each two separated by alternately large and small picots, and you should have a square (g). Now produce an oval (h) and a more complex square with graded picots (i). Make some asymmetrical shapes (j and k).

By now we can be said to have explored the decorative use of the picot fairly thoroughly although, obviously, there are endless variations. So back to rings.

Shapes of more than one ring

Make a ring of twelve double knots, close it. With the same continuing thread make another ring hard by the first ring, make a third ring and finish off by knotting the two ends of thread together (l) and finish off. Make a shape with four rings (m), five (n) and six (o).

The picot as joining agent

We are now beginning to see what shapes transpire out of rings alone. However, at this stage they handle sloppily, so let us now exploit the picot as a joining and stabilizing agent, as well as decoration (p, q, r, s): Make a ring composed of 2 double knots, 1 small picot, 4 double knots, 1 small picot, 1 double knot, 1 large picot, 1 double knot, 1 small picot, 4 double knots, 1 small picot, 2 double knots, close the ring.* Start the next ring hard by, make 2 double knots, then insert the hook or point of the shuttle or a small crochet hook into the last picot of the last ring, catch the thread on the hook and pull it through the picot until there is a loop large enough to take the shuttle. Put the shuttle through this loop and then pull the

c

loop back again until the thread it leaves just lies snugly over the running-line of the present ring without distorting it. *This movement always counts as one half of a double knot*, so make the second half. Make 3 double knots, 1 small picot, 1 double knot, 1 large picot, 1 double knot, 1 small picot, 4 double knots,* 1 small picot, 2 double knots, close the ring. Repeat from * to *. We are now going to join the last ring to the first ring. Put the hook through the first picot of the first ring, catch the running-line of the present ring on the hook and draw it through sufficiently to take the shuttle, put the shuttle through, pull the loop thread back until it is just lying nicely over the running-line without distorting it, do one and a half more double knots, close the ring, tie the first and last ends of thread at the back and finish off. The last double knots after a first and last ring have been joined are quite tricky to make and need some dexterous manipulation. We now have *p*, an improved version of *l*, stable and decorative, and *m*, *n* and *o* can be treated in a like manner to make *q*, *r* and *s*. (Note that in each of these the picots as decoration have been treated differently.) When producing these shapes as soon as more than three rings are incorporated in the shape, they must have a small space of thread left between them at the base to allow them to settle properly.

We now have, in addition to all else, used rings to form the basic tatting shapes, the triangle, square, pentagon and hexagon, and one could continue with 7 ring shapes, 8 ring shapes and so on.

Basic shapes formed into fabric

The next logical step is to take the basic shapes we have made and, by placing them end to end, form them into edgings or strips of fabric which can be combined with cloth, ribbon and even soft leather and suede.

In fig. 43, *a* is the triangle formed into a strip of fabric; *b* and *c* are strips of fabric formed from the square in two different ways; *d* is a pentagon formed into a strip of fabric, but in this case a straight line is impossible; *e* is the hexagon formed into a strip of fabric.

When forming motifs into strips, join motif to motif as follows: make one motif, make the second motif leaving the actual joining until the last ring or rings of the second motif are being produced, tat up to the point where the join is to be made, place motif to motif and join as usual via the picot.

We have now produced five different designs suitable for edgings, but from these basic shapes one can make areas of fabric which can be as extensive as you wish (see fig. 44): *a* and *d* use the triangle (or diamond formed of two triangles) put together in two different ways; *b* uses the square; *c* the hexagon.

Fig. 43
Tatting with one thread: basic shapes as strips of fabric.

a

b

c

d

e

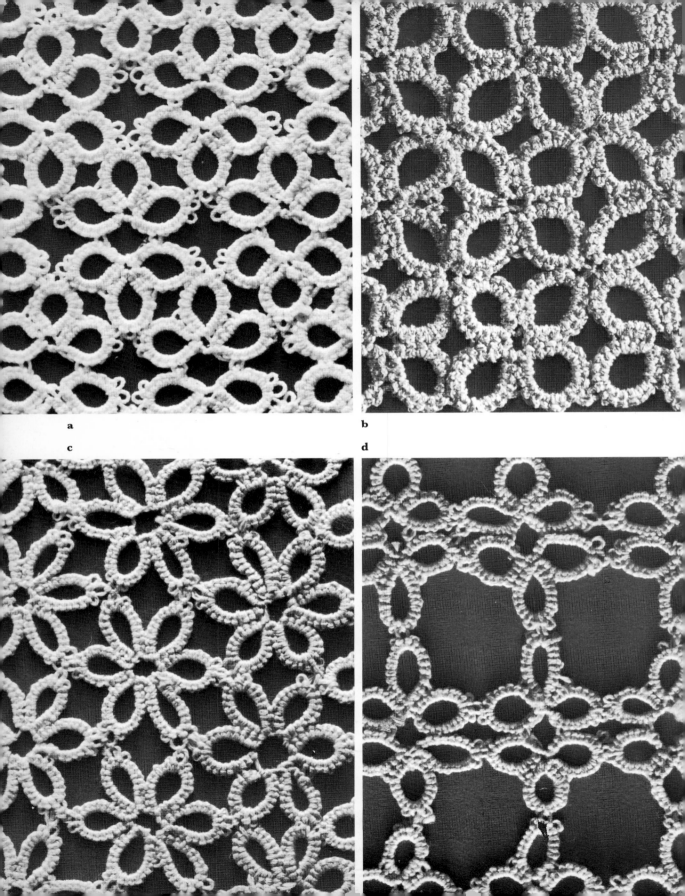

a

b

c

d

Fig. 44
Tatting with one thread: basic shapes
forming fabric.

A pentagon will not form flat fabric on its own, but the end-papers of the book show how pentagons may be used to cover an extended area in a three-dimensional form.

Tatting instructions

From this point on, the abbreviations given on page 8 will be used in instructions. It should be noted also that you can follow a tatting pattern from a piece of work or a good photograph (hence the magnifying glass illustrated in fig. 28).

The ring as a stable centre to a motif

As you will have found, the bigger a shape made of rings becomes, the less stable is its centre. There is a way of both stabilizing the centre and making it decorative.

In fig. 45, *a* is made as follows:

Ring   2 dk, (p, 3 dk) × 5, p, 1 dk, cr. With a hook draw the shuttle thread through the nearest picot, put the shuttle through and pull up into a tight knot.

*Ring   3 dk, p, 3 dk, lp, 2 dk, lp, 3 dk, p, 3 dk, cr. With the hook, draw the shuttle thread through the next picot, put the shuttle through, pull tight, repeat from * five times, joining the rings together and the first ring to the last ring at the appropriate picots. Finish off.

We have now produced a motif with a firm, stable centre, a very traditional formation known as a 'daisy' (already seen in fig. 27*b*). *b* is another variation.

This has brought us to another traditional formation, the 'wheel' (*c*) (already seen in fig. 27*c*).

Fig. 45
Tatting with one thread: the ring as
centre to a motif.

a   b   c

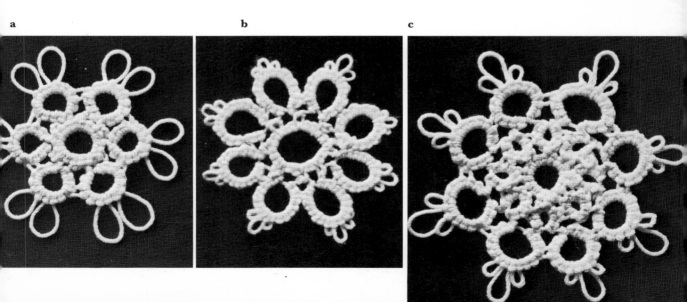

This was made as follows:

Ring 1 dk, (p, 1 dk) × 8, cr. Finish off.

With a new thread:

Ring 3 dk, p, 4 dk, p, 1 dk, lp, 1 dk, p, 4 dk, p, 3 dk, cr, tw.

Ring 2 dk, p, 2 dk, join to p of centre r, on wrong side, 2 dk, p, 2 dk, cr, tw.

*Ring 3 dk, join to last picot of previous large ring, 4 dk, p, 1 dk, lp, 1 dk, p, 4 dk, p, 3 dk, cr, tw.

Ring 2 dk, join to last p of previous small r, 2 dk, join to next picot of central r on wrong side, 2 dk, p, 2 dk, cr, tw.

Repeat from * 6 times.

Join the first large ring to the last large ring. Finish off.

If the centre ring has a large picot between every double knot, these can be caught together in threes for making the succeeding round of rings, thus forming a star-like shape in the centre.

By now we are dealing with some fairly complex formations. On the way we have made isolated motifs, small and large strips of fabric and areas of fabric. We shall now return to the concept of the simple ring, at the same time utilizing spaces of unworked thread.

Half rings

If we adopt the simple means of making a ring, but instead of drawing it up tightly as we have until now, leave some of the ring or running-line exposed and unworked, we achieve a half ring. Half rings will automatically form strips instead of motifs.

In fig. 46:

A strip formed of half rings of 12 dk (*a*).

As *a*, but embellished with picots (*b*).

A strip of half rings embellished and joined with picots (*c*).

Half rings standing on either side of the centre (*d*).

Half rings into a circle (*e*).

Half rings, standing on either side of the centre, made into fabric (*f*).

Rings used as a continuous line

If we make complete, drawn-up rings once again, but instead of making the second ring close or near to the first, leave an unworked space of thread, this frees the rings of the tendency to form into shapes so that they can be used as continuous strips. To get the spaces exact if they are large, measure the thread and put a pin at the point where the next ring will start.

In fig. 46:

A strip composed of rings of 12 dk and 4 dk, the latter known as an oillet (*g*).

A strip composed of rings decorated with picots (*h*).

As *h*, but joined by picots (*i*).

Fig. 46
Tatting with one thread: lengths of unworked thread.

The rings stand on either side of the thread (j).

Like f, j and g can obviously be made into a very open fabric, becoming 'mignonette stitch' or 'tatting ground stitch'. The study of rings used in this manner, i.e. with spaces of unworked thread left in between, leads us directly on to working with two threads, since it is possible with two threads to cover the lengths of unworked thread with double knots.

5 Working with two threads, the line

Working with two threads enlarges the scope of designing enormously, as one is released from the necessity of making both knot and running-line from the same length of thread and thus of constantly producing rings, or rings and spaces of unworked thread. With two threads, one as the running-line and the other as the knot, one can make free moving lines and move from one point in the work to another without hindrance. When the technique was discovered, its first use was to move from ring to ring more freely and to create a more attractive effect. But to design really creatively, it is well to forget rings and to forget working with one thread for the moment and to turn, instead, to working with two threads almost as if the process were unrelated, thus using it as a productive design force entirely in its own right. Working with one thread *and* two is dealt with in chapter 6.

Preparing the threads

When working with two threads, there are various methods of preparation:

1. One thread comes from the shuttle, the other from the ball. Before beginning knot the two together by means of a tight reef-knot with the ends snipped off close. (NB: the knot can be messy and obtrusive if the yarn is a heavy one.)

2. Wind the shuttle without cutting the thread from the ball, so as to dispense with the joining knot. Make a small overhand knot in the thread just to give one a starting point and something for the finger and thumb to hold on to.

3. Wind two shuttles and knot the two threads together as before. Working with two shuttles is an advantage over ball and shuttle as they can act as running-line or knot in turn.

4. Wind one shuttle, then remove an equivalent length of thread from the ball and wind on to the second shuttle. This leaves no break in the thread, merely a small overhand knot to pinpoint the start.

5. Either wind two shuttles, or wind one shuttle and use the ball-thread. With the shuttle thread, start the work with a ring, turn the work upside down, pass the second thread through the ring and knot it once tightly between the first and last stitches of the ring. There are now two ends and two threads. While working the ensuing line, pull the two ends through three double knots as they are made and before they are tightened. Cut the ends off.*

Knotting

To begin practical work, for now use method 2. Wind a shuttle without cutting the thread from the ball, and make a small overhand knot in the thread 7 inches (18 cm.) from the shuttle. Hold the knot between forefinger and thumb of the left hand with the shuttle hanging down, and wind the ball thread over the fingers of the left hand (fig. 47).

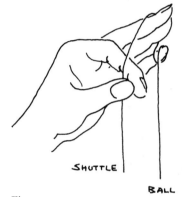

Fig. 47

This tensioning of the ball thread over the fingers of the left hand is very important and requires getting used to before proceeding. Take the shuttle in the right hand and with the shuttle make the usual movements for the double knot, allowing the ball thread to take over as the actual knot. Make the first knot hard against the overhand knot starting point. Continue to knot. You will find that the work takes on a natural curve, see fig. 48a. Now, quite deliberately, try to make a length of straight line (b). Use a locking stitch first, i.e. a half knot which does not 'turn' and therefore locks the passage of the running-line. You will find that to make a straight line you will have to manipulate the knots into place. Now make twelve double knots, allowing natural curve as before, then twelve knots with the *shuttle thread knotting over the ball thread* (having learnt how to 'turn' the tatting double knot, it is quite difficult to return to this simple, unturned knot). Make twelve double knots proper and twelve double knots unturned (c). Now repeat this last exercise but after each twelve knots pull up whichever thread is acting as the running-line very tightly to produce d (do not forget to use locking stitches where necessary). Make twelve double knots, pull the work up tightly, turn the work (turn it over, top to bottom), repeat this five times (e). Make

---

*As described in *Tatting* by B. Attenborough, page 20. The method can also be used for joining in new thread while working.

Fig. 48
Tatting with two threads and one shuttle: the line.

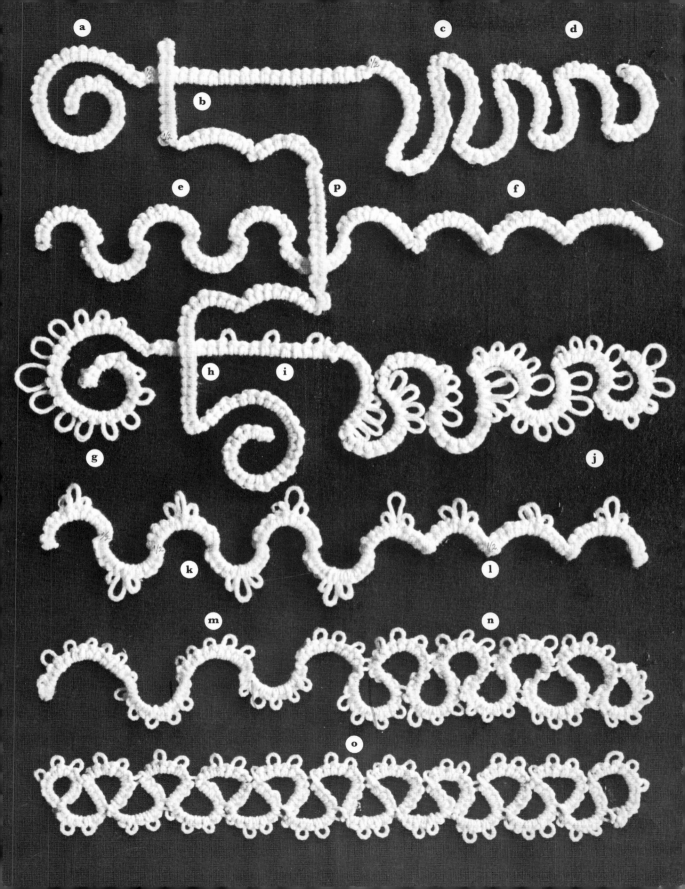

twelve double knots, pull the running-line tightly, make one locking stitch, repeat three times (*f*). Produce *a–f* embellished with picots (*g–l*).

Now use picots to join sections (*n*), a natural outcome of *k* (push the work up close and join at the appropriate picots).

To produce *m*:
Line   4 dk, (p, 2 dk) × 5, 2 dk, tw, rep 5 times.

To produce *n*:
4 dk, join to last picot of last line but one, 2 dk, (p, 2 dk) × 4, 2 dk, tw, rep 7 times.

o is made as follows:

With ball and shuttle as before but with *one* thread:
Ring   4 dk, (p, 2 dk) × 4, 2 dk, cr, tw.
With two threads:
Line   2 dk, (p, 2 dk) × 3, 2 dk, join into last picot of r, tw.
Line   2 dk, (p, 2 dk) × 3, 2 dk, join to last picot of previous line, tw, continue.

Having got this far it is a good exercise to make a free drawing and follow its lines faithfully by means of the line (*p*).

Working with two shuttles

When working, as we have been, with one shuttle and the remaining thread on the ball, if we use the orthodox tatting double knot then the shuttle thread can never be other than the running-line and the ball thread never other than the knot. Working with two shuttles gives one greater freedom, as either thread can be the running-line or the knot. Otherwise, with only one shuttle, we cannot make the shuttle thread into the knot other than by using the unturned knot described on page 42. Having once mastered the correct tatting double knot, it is really preferable to keep to it. One only has to resort to the unorthodox method if one has no second shuttle or if, when working in extremely thick thread, one wishes all parts of the work to face the same way to hide the backs of picots. This latter use is really its greatest value.

With two shuttles wound, make a line of ten double knots with the first shuttle, turn the work, make a line of ten double knots with the second shuttle, turn the work, repeat three times (fig. 49*a*). Compare this with fig. 48*e* and you will see the changing point is neater because each thread can now remain in its own place.

Now with the first shuttle:
Line   2 dk, p, 6 dk, p, 2 dk, tw, repeat with the second shuttle, tw.

Fig. 49
Tatting with two threads and two shuttles: the line.

Again with the first shuttle:

2 dk, join to last picot of first ~~line~~ [chain], 6 dk, p, 2 dk, tw.

With the second shuttle:

2 dk, join to last picot of second ~~line~~ [chain], 6 dk, p, 2 dk, tw, continue.

These are a form of 'mock-rings', i.e. they are beginning to look like rings but are in fact lines (b). c is the mock-ring embellished with picots. Obviously, as before, this formation can be made into fabric as well as strips (d).

Another form of mock-ring is produced when a ~~line~~ [chain] is joined to a picot made at the start, thus forming a ring. This can go straight on to another ~~line~~ [chain], something a one-shuttle ring cannot do (e).

A mock-ring with picots can form the centre of a shape made with ~~lines~~ [chains] (f) which can have the bases of its semicircles open not closed.

g and h are both variations on this theme, having a picot-bearing mock-ring as the centre and picot-bearing ~~lines~~ [chains] as the succeeding rounds. The first round is made straight on from the mock-ring but succeeding rounds have to be started with new threads.

From the foregoing, it is clear that working with two threads producing only the ~~line~~ [chain] has a design force in its own right. Shapes and areas result which are of a different nature and visual impact to those produced when making rings with one thread (see puppet in fig. 89).

i is traditionally called 'node stitch'. It is three (or four, or more) half-hitches and three reversed half-hitches repeated. It is inserted here because it is useful for making a really straight ~~line~~ [chain]. It takes the formation of a straight ~~line~~ [chain] easily because the heads of the knots are single not double and do not lie on one side but around the running ~~line~~ [chain]. The Josephine ~~line~~ [chain] (j) is equally useful for straight ~~lines~~ [chains], being composed of half-hitches only.

6 Working with two threads, rings and lines together

Tatting is at its most versatile when it is produced by two shuttles working freely, with either shuttle producing rings or lines. It is a good idea to use two shuttles which can be differentiated from each other. In the instructions that follow it is assumed that the same shuttle is being used for the knotting until the second shuttle is mentioned. When the second shuttle takes over as the knotting shuttle instead of supplying the running-line, directions say 'with the second shuttle'.

The only reason for dealing with lines in isolation in the last chapter was to establish rings and lines as equal design factors and not, as so often happens, lines used merely as a means of joining rings together. However, this was undoubtedly their first function and we will now return to this use of them.

In fig. 39, motifs *q*, *r* and *s* are worked with small spaces of thread left between and at the base of the rings. In small motifs the unworked threads look well but in larger motifs they can be replaced by lines as in fig. 50*a*.

This is made as follows:

Ring   2 dk, p, 5 dk, p, 1 dk, lp, 1 dk, p, 5 dk, p, 2 dk, cr, tw.
Line   2 dk, p, 2 dk, tw.

Continue, joining at the first and last picots of each ring. Further motifs *g*, *h*, *i* and *j* in fig. 46 can all be produced with lines instead of unworked thread as in fig. 50*b*, *c* and *d*.

b is produced as follows:

Ring   5 dk, p, 1 dk, lp, 1 dk, p, 5 dk, cr, tw.
Line   6 dk, tw, continue.

c is a much-used formation, traditionally known as a scroll:

Ring   12 dk, cr, tw.
Line   12 dk, tw, continue.

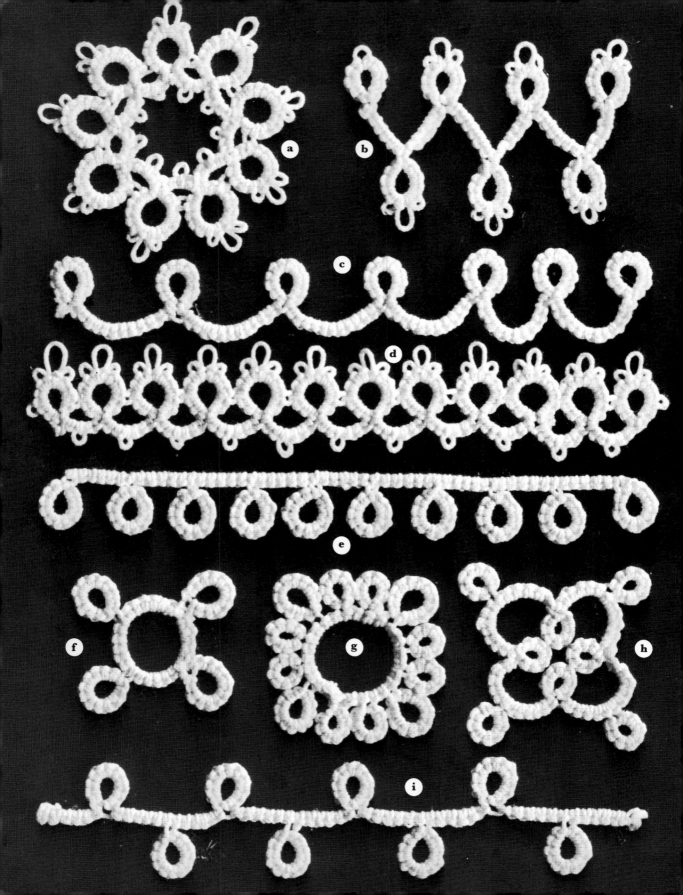

Fig. 50
Tatting with two threads: rings and
lines together.

d elaborates the scroll principle:

Ring   3 dk, p, 3 dk, p, 1 dk, lp, 1 dk, p, 3 dk, p, 3 dk, cr, tw.
Line   3 dk, p, 3 dk, tw.

Continue, joining at the first and last picots of every ring.

e is produced as follows:
With the first shuttle:
Ring   12 dk, cr.
With the second shuttle:
Line   6 dk, continue.

Here we see that the running-line is a continuous thread through the lines and the rings stand on this line. This is a very useful technique if a piece of tatting is to be fitted around a piece of cloth or a shape since the running-line can be drawn up as desired – see *f* and *g*. If the shuttles making the rings are alternated, the rings can stand on either side of the lines, *h* and *i*.

It would be pointless to categorize design possibilities further. It is up to the individual designer to pursue her own creative ideas.

D

7 Varying the approach

Introducing colour
In any piece of tatting made with two shuttles, two different colours can be used. It follows therefore that in any piece of finished work composed of smaller elements a considerable number of colours could be incorporated.

Using different thread sizes
Tatting made with two shuttles can be produced with a heavy thread on one shuttle and a fine thread on the other. Fine thread, knotting over a heavy running-line, and heavy thread knotting over a fine running-line can have interesting textural qualities.

Designing one's own threads
Should the exact shade and thickness of thread required be unavailable, a composite thread can be composed of as many as two, three or four finer ones of varying colours and lustres. These should be knotted and wound together most carefully on to the shuttle (e.g. no. 24 in fig. 1).

Introducing texture
In essence, tatting requires strong, fine, tightly twisted, lustrous, non-hairy yarns, and these should certainly be used by the beginner. But once you are proficient with the technique, it is important to experiment with threads, making trial samples. Some excessively frail or textured yarns cannot be used but it is surprising what seemingly unsuitable yarns turn out to be successful.

Having learned the basics of tatting in an average size thread, work in Sylko to cultivate a sense of the miniature, in jute to obtain the gigantic, in a fine metallic yarn to obtain the jewel-like, in tapestry wool to get the soft and full, and in 'Novacord' to get the crisp and sturdy.

Combining tatting with other textile constructions

There is absolutely no reason at all why the basic structure of a piece of work should be entirely of tatting. Other textile techniques, like crochet, knitting, macramé and knotting are all suitable complementary constructions, and can sometimes be integrated into the whole design conception to provide areas of contrasting texture.

Combining tatting with other materials

The materials with which tatting is most often combined, and with which we are most familiar, are linens, cottons and their man-made equivalents. These, of course, are correct and proper for objects which are to be laundered frequently. However, many other materials, depending entirely upon the texture and tactile quality of the tatting, can be aesthetically right, like soft suedes and leathers, felts and synthetic leather and plastics, velvets, nets, hand-weaving, and many others. Some of these fabrics have the added attraction of unfrayable edges, which is useful where tatting is attached to rather than placed on the fabric. Work of this nature can sometimes only be dry-cleaned, not laundered, and therefore it may be best to conceive the design in rich, lustrous colours. Ribbons and braids link well with strips of tatting to form areas of fabric.

Mounting tatting

Tatting can be mounted on wood, card, felt, velvet, suede, and on or between sheets of glass or perspex (see fig. 86). This generally means that its function as fabric, except in a textural sense, has ceased and therefore the design can be freed of the demands imposed by a functional textile (see fig. 2).

Tatting with beads

Beads are strung on to the thread which will form the final double knot. (It is easier if this is the ball-thread.) The beads are manipulated into place as and when desired, positioned on picots between the heads of the double knots.

When beading on rings, thread the beads on to the shuttle thread as it is wound. Bring the number of beads required for a ring up and on to the circle of thread around the left hand, leaving them out of the way near the little finger. Work the required number of double knots then slide a bead up the thread into the position of the picot and work your next double knot thus trapping the bead.

To work strings of rings and beads, make a ring of half the required double knots, then measure your picot against the bead and make it slightly longer, finish the next double knots and close the ring, and finish off. When making the next ring pull the picot of the first ring through the hole in the bead and join to the second ring at its beginning, make the ring as before and close.

Tatting with very heavy thread

Tatting can be produced with the fingers if extremely heavy thread is used (fig. 87). In general, heavy threads bring to the fore something which is not apparent or important in finer work, i.e. the break in the heads of knots seen on the back of the fabric where picots occur. If necessary, this can be prevented by using the unturned double knot already referred to on page 42. Instead of turning the work upside down in order to produce lines, the work remains face up in the hands and the line is a series of unturned, instead of turned, knots. This method was, in fact, used long ago and discarded in favour of the constant use of the turned double knot but there is good reason for its revival in the production of some heavy work.

Areas of unworked thread

Assuming that the thread itself is sufficiently attractive, areas of unworked thread can produce open, net-like fabric (fig. 75), or form part of a free graphic conception (fig. 40).

Three-dimensional work

Three-dimensional tatting results when there are insufficient knots, rings or lines to allow the work to remain flat. Three-dimensional work is illustrated in the endpapers.

8 Finishing processes

Securing the ends

When producing small samples of work, such as those illustrated in chapters 4, 5 and 6, it is quick and sufficient to secure the ends of the threads with a very sparing dab of a glue suitable for fabric. To use any other method on small pieces with many ends which only serve as experimental work and have no functional purpose is laborious and time-wasting. Knotting the ends together is sometimes employed for the production of trial samples, but can be bulky and looks untidy. Adhesive can also be used when tatting is a means of abstract expression and where the fabric no longer has a practical function.

However, when we consider tatting as a functional textile it is best to apply the following procedure. First work out the total design carefully on paper so that all joining-points are foreseen, and make all joins via picots. Where ends occur, knot the two ends together *once* and then thread each end singly into a sewing needle and draw it through the back of two or three double knots, one to the left and one to the right. Snip the ends off close. Another method is to sew the two ends down, one by one, with fine sewing thread. Remember that tatting is very strong and neat until ends occur, so ending-off must be equally strong and neat.

Blocking

Constructed textiles, whether woven, knitted or whatever, are often still unfinished when the final stitch or knot is made. The threads have been formed into complex constructions by means of fingers and tools but they need to 'settle down'. We all know how threads can twist and curl, how knitting can roll up, and so on.

When considering how to finish remember that when fibre is dry it is self-willed, when it is wet it is malleable, and the heavier the yarn the more it imposes its own will. With very fine tatting the knot and general construction is dominant over the thread so that the thread will stay in position. Therefore, assuming it is clean, the tatting may need nothing more than a very gentle pressing. However with work composed of heavier yarns the fabric is washed by being gently squeezed between the fingers in warm, soapy water (*never rub*). Rinse in warm water until the water is clear, then squeeze it out by hand. Any further moisture is removed by wrapping the fabric in a towel and squeezing. Throughout this process the yarns must not be treated harshly or flattened. Now give the piece of work a gentle shake and place it on the blocking pad (see fig. 28), a pad of soft pin-board, such as 'Celotex', with a squared paper surface covered with strong, clear plastic. Now pin the work carefully into its correct shape using lots of rustless pins, pinning every picot, and utilizing the measured squares as guide lines to the size, shape and the correct vertical and horizontal. If necessary, instead of washing, the work can be pinned on to the blocking-pad first and then sprinkled with water, but obviously water does not penetrate so well this way. When it is bone dry, take it off the pad: the work holds the shape into which it has been pinned. Starch may be applied if desired.

This process has been followed to achieve stability and shape and to make the threads swell and settle down into place. The removal of dirt has been almost incidental. Should the work have become dirty or stained, then the appropriate stronger washing agents can be used instead of soap. Obviously, one tries to keep it as clean as possible while it is being produced, but this is remarkably difficult as tatting is constantly between the fingers.

Pressing with an iron has only been mentioned in connection with fine thread because the last thing we want to do is flatten the work, which may occur when ironing heavier thread. When heavy tatting is laundered later on in its life it should again be blocked. Otherwise press it *very* lightly and gently on the wrong side with a damp cloth and into a soft ironing blanket, with a fairly hot iron, aiming more at a steaming than a pressing process.

Protection against dirt

A fabric protector finish (such as 'Scotchgard') will protect work against air and water-borne soiling and spillage. Treated fabric can be laundered as usual and should be treated again in time (directions on the canister). Spraying with a protector finish is particularly useful if tatting is to be applied un-protected to something like a light fitting which can never be cleaned or laundered.

How to attach tatting to fabric

Attaching to a fabric edge

If the fabric is suede, leather, felt or plastic, then use a large darning needle to make or mark a row of holes along the edge of the fabric $\frac{1}{8}$ inch (3 mm.) from the edge and as far apart as the picots that will be used to join the edge of the tatting. If the fabric is a knitted or crocheted one then the necessary holes will be in the construction of the fabric itself. If the fabric is a woven one a small $\frac{1}{8}$ inch (3 mm.) hem should be made on the edge, preferably hem-stitched to produce regular and accurate holes. Attach the tatting, if possible, while it is being made. Begin by drawing the doubled free end of the tatting thread, which is wound on the shuttle, through the first hole in the fabric, put the shuttle through the resulting loop and pull tight. Now tat until the next joining point is reached. Draw the thread through the next hole, put the shuttle thread through the loop, pull tight, and so on. If for some reason the tatting cannot be attached while it is being made, use a fine sewing thread or invisible nylon sewing thread to attach the tatting to the fabric with one or two small stitches at the joining points, which could well be a picot, then run the needle and thread through the hem, bringing it up at the next joining point. Tatting can be attached with an embroidery stitch, buttonhole stitch often being used, but you should decide from a design point of view whether this second element is desirable or whether it will be distracting.

Inserting into fabric

Almost always the piece of tatting will have been produced and completed before being attached to fabric. In this case use one of the following methods.

1. With the blocking-pad as a base, lay the tatting on the fabric and pin (straight in, do not have the pins at an angle). With a sharp, hard pencil draw around the edge of the tatting shape on the fabric but inside the rows of double knots. When the tatting is removed we shall see a shape on the fabric which is a 'row of double knots' width' smaller than the piece of tatting. If the fabric is a frayable one, with a sewing machine make a narrow overlocking or zig-zag stitch just outside the pencil lines. If the fabric is leather, suede or felt, this will not be needed. Cut away the resulting shape. Place the tatting

over the cut area and sew down over the overlocked lines, with invisible nylon sewing thread, obtainable from dress-makers' shops.

2. Lay the tatting on the fabric as before, draw an outline beyond the tatting and touching the picots. Buttonhole-stitch around the shape, with the same thread as the tatting, catching the picots in the buttonholing as you come to them. Overlocking on a machine can be used instead, the picots being caught into this afterwards by invisible nylon sewing thread.

Method 1 leaves the tatting design unaltered, method 2 adds another element, an outline, which may or may not be desirable.

Attaching to fabric
Place the work on the backing fabric, tack into place, and sew on with invisible nylon thread. Assuming that the back of the fabric will not be seen, the tatting ends, instead of being threaded through the double knots, can be left and finally taken through to the back of the backing fabric and fastened off there.

Preserving tatting

If the work is used entirely as a fine-art concept, with no practical textile purpose except the visual, it can be given various spray finishes to help it resist ageing and dirt and to give it body. Thinned varnishes and lacquers will give a solid, permanent protection but may impart shine – spray a trial piece first. P.V.A. (UK), or Hyplar (USA) diluted with 50% water and sprayed through a hair spray or the like several times will harden the work completely and make it solid and sculptural. Let one spraying dry before applying the next. (For example, see fig. 87.)

It is fair to assume that jewelry and ornament produced in tatting will not be subjected to rough or even constant usage and will never need washing. Therefore it is sometimes desirable either because of the character of the yarn used, or in the interests of neatness, to use an adhesive as a means of securing ends, rather than threading the ends through. Use one which does not change its colour, such as P.V.A. or Hyplar, and spray with 'Scotchgard'.

Mounting and framing work

If a piece of work is a purely abstract fine-art concept, the material on to which it is mounted will undoubtedly have been part of the initial design decision and may well be perspex (plexiglass), glass, plastics, fabric of any sort, metal, wood, card or any of a myriad number of materials. The work will be held with either stitches, or adhesives. Embroiderers and textile artists now have to make two deliberate decisions, whether to put the work beneath glass for protection or not and whether a frame is required or not. Occasionally it is an integral part of the design concept to trap work between glass or perspex, in which case there is no problem. My own feeling is that to put a textile beneath glass is undesirable and it is preferable to spray the work with a protective finish and accept that it is vulnerable to time. However, sometimes a client will intervene, who insists on glass being used. There is a glass available called 'diffused reflection glass' (see suppliers) which is better than the normal product but expensive.

With glass a problem arises of holding it in place. If a frame is considered unnecessary there are clips available which are reasonably but not totally unobtrusive. However after a long time dirt may intrude at the edges, particularly as tatting has depth and should not be flattened. In order to avoid these problems a fillet can be placed around the work between glass and mount. Properly, frames should *always* be part of the total design concept, never an afterthought. One can rarely procure a mass-produced frame which is just right and it is more likely that one will employ a specialist framer or carpenter. It may be that a simple perspex or natural wood frame is all that is required, or it may be appropriate to cover a frame in, or make the frame of, one of the fabric elements of the design, thus drawing it completely into the total concept.

It may be that the fabric on which the tatting is placed needs to be stretched to produce a totally even surface. If so, cut a piece of card a little smaller than the finished measurements to allow for the fabric thickness at the edges. Place the fabric face down on a clean board with the card upon it. Bring over one long edge, lining the card up accurately with the threads (if it is a woven fabric) and glue. Now smooth the fabric firmly across the card, bring over the opposite edge and glue, again lining up the threads. Now decide what to do about the corners: fine fabrics can be folded down into place and non-fraying fabrics can be mitred; heavy, frayable fabrics can be carefully mitred if fabric glue is first smeared on the back of the fabric and allowed to dry before cutting. Now line up and glue down the first short side, then smooth the fabric across the card and glue the second short side. There should not be even a suspicion of a wrinkle.

Tatting can be attached to its base fabric with sparing applications of adhesive. If adhesive does not seem appropriate choose a card mount which is just light enough to stitch through. Try not to attach tatting to a base fabric before the fabric is stretched or the tatting may distort when the base fabric is stretched over the card mount. If for some reason it *is* necessary to attach the work to the base fabric before the latter is stretched on the card, then stretch the fabric carefully in an embroidery frame, or the like, while working.

9 Design sources and media

Fig. 51
Two sketches, one of rocks on Capri, the other of Warwick Castle, both containing useful design material.

Today, materials and techniques, whether clay is being made into pots, yarn into weaving, or metal fashioned into shapes, have two functions. They can be used in a totally practical and functional manner to produce cups, cloth and implements, or they can be used to bring abstract concepts into tangible existence. Artists have always used paint, wood, stone and metal to give life to their thoughts but the use of materials, fibre and thread to this abstract end is, on the whole, a more contemporary concept.

The two aspects, practical and abstract, have more than materials and technique in common, namely an aesthetic role, intrinsic in art objects but sometimes ignored in practical work. For this content we draw on the natural world more often than we know, for design ideas and visual source material are all around us. It is helpful to most of us to record those things that excite us visually rather than carry them in our heads. The drawing-pad and the camera are both the tool of the designer at this stage. When drawing, the implements most allied to the sense of thread, and tatting in particular, are rapidographs or the like and fibre tipped pens, which give a clean line and can move easily and quickly over the page. In fig. 51 are two landscape sketches (one in rapidograph, one in fibre pen) not intended to be followed literally but parts of which were used later in various pieces of work. Fig. 52 shows a Heath Robinson illustration to a poem (*b*), and *a* and *c* are both traced scraps from an old book of fairy tales. Fig. 53 shows a drawing of a poplar tree intended directly for tatting.

The camera can be used in two ways, either to record something for later development when there is no time for drawing, or it can be used as creatively as the drawing-pad and pen – a design tool in its own right. In figs. 54 and 55 are photographs of interesting subject matter, and fig. 56 indicates how

a

b

c

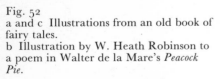

Fig. 52
a and c Illustrations from an old book of
fairy tales.
b Illustration by W. Heath Robinson to
a poem in Walter de la Mare's *Peacock
Pie*.

Fig. 53
Drawing of a poplar tree.

opposite page
Fig. 54
Old fish-boxes and rope (photograph,
Irene Waller).

a

b

c

d

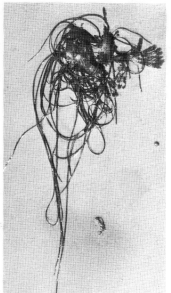

Fig. 56
Seaweed changing in form as it is
washed by each successive wave
(photographs, Geoffrey Waller).

important it is to get to know one's subject thoroughly when
photographing. The art of drawing familiarizes one with the
subject automatically, but the camera does not necessarily
do so.

As well as drawing and photography, the study of objects
in books, magazines, exhibitions and museums, galleries and
churches, is all food for the designer and should be collected
for reference when needed.

Once the initial idea has been conceived, recorded and
developed, the technique must then be considered. After that,
the job of organizing a design for a particular piece of work
can be undertaken in any of the ways indicated in the next
chapter.

opposite page
Fig. 55
a Indian palisades, Lake Huron,
Canada.
b Exterior of Indian longhouse,
Ontario, Canada.
c Seaweed.
d Jesuit missionary palisades, Lake
Huron, Canada (photographs, Irene
Waller).

10 Organizing design

In all textile media, before totally free creative work can be achieved, the technical aspect of the chosen form of construction should have been thoroughly absorbed and understood. Having learned and practised the basic technique and the ways in which it can be explored, then the artist and designer can apply this information creatively. Otherwise, she does not necessarily recognize the full potential of the medium she has chosen.

Once the initial idea has been conceived and developed, and the method of construction considered, the technical part of organizing the design can be undertaken in any of the following ways:

1. Fig. 57a shows a mock-up, at the idea stage, of a design suitable for the neck area of a garment – possibly a blouse, a dress or a kaftan. It uses fabric, threads, beads and paillettes and is glued on to card. Fig. 57b shows the finished object. The design was not slavishly followed; rather, one continues to develop one's idea right the way through a piece of work to the end. The neck edge is a scroll, then rings of various sizes and yarns were produced, joined together by picots.

2. Experiments in three-dimensional work on spheres (fig. 58a) led to decorative baubles (fig. 58b) and a necklace (fig. 79). Designs were drawn on to the polystyrene spheres and then reproduced in the tatting.

3. When creating body-jewelry or parts of garments, a dressmaker's stand is absolutely invaluable as the main elements of the design can be pinned into place and the linking elements designed around them. The work illustrated in fig. 80 was all made on the stand included among the equipment in fig. 28.

4. When designing a repeating pattern composed of rings, or shapes composed of rings, first decide upon the size of the

Fig. 57
a Mock-up on card in yarns, beads and fabric for blouse neck design.
b Finished piece of work.

a

b

Fig. 58
a Tatting worked over polystyrene
spheres, on which the design was drawn,
and over marbles.
b Christmas baubles, worked in the
same manner.

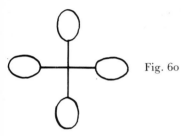

Fig. 59

Fig. 60

ring (fig. 59), then upon the size and character of the shape (fig. 60). Trace this motif ten or twelve times, cut around these roughly. Place these in juxtaposition to one another, and rearrange until the required effect is obtained (fig. 61). Then, if necessary, fill in spaces with further shapes. Mark all points where picots are needed both for ornament and particularly for joining (fig. 62). Then make a sample ring of double knots in the chosen thread, place this on the drawn motif and note where picots must come (fig. 63). One is then ready to begin the work proper. The fabric in fig. 64 is the result. (It was found that with only one double knot at either end of the ring the last large picot twisted, so the ring was modified.) Working instructions are as follows:

With a shuttle thread and a ball thread:
Ring   2 dk, lp, 2 dk, (1 p, 2 dk) × 5, lp, 2 dk, cr, tw.
Line   4 dk, 1 p, 4 dk.
Ring As before.
Line   4 dk, attach to picot of previous l, 4 dk.*
Rep from * to * twice. Fasten off.

Fig. 61

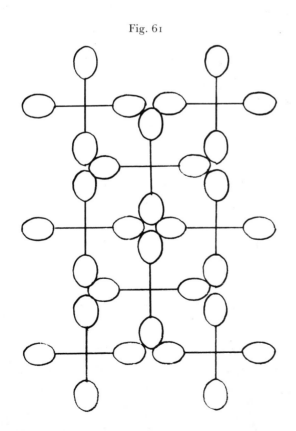

Fig. 62

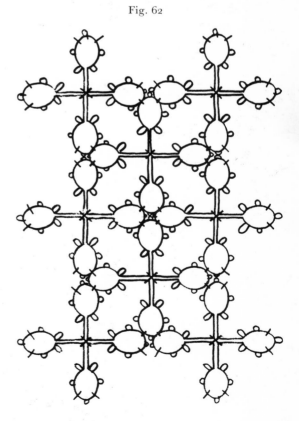

Fig. 63

Fig. 64

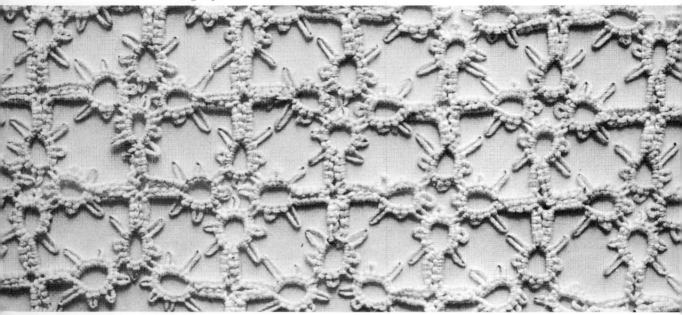

When producing further motifs, attach at the appropriate picots.

Follow the same general principles, as far as picots and joining are concerned, when designing freer forms.

When planning shaped pieces of tatting for garments or objects, the plan of the tatted fabric on tracing paper (as on page 67) can be placed over a paper pattern and thus the tatting related totally to the garment with the motifs at the shaped edges reshaped accordingly.

There are pattern books available which are a fund of ideas and instructions but one should use these to one's own ends, adapting basic shapes and patterns to one's own creative requirements.

It is a good idea to procure a big, hard-covered, loose-leaf file to contain one's drawings, notes and samples of work. With black card pages with acetate or clear plastic page covers, writing paper and drawing paper, one can keep practical work tidily and cleanly together with notes and drawings (see fig. 28).

One final but important word about designing. To many people who do not have the benefit of a design training the word 'design' is often frightening, or even pretentious. There is really no need to take this view because, put simply, good design is what pleases the discerning eye and mind.

The way of overcoming an inhibition about 'design' is firstly to learn one's craft thoroughly so that it is the servant and not the master, and then, when its natural forms are taking shape in one's fingers, consider the visual and tactile effects of the emerging work in a critical manner. A pinboard is invaluable for this. Acquire a piece of white pinboarding and have it fixed to a wall. Paint one half of it a soft dark colour and the other half white so that you have a light area against which to assess dark work and vice versa. Now pin the work to it and consider whether it pleases you or not. Generally one's eye tells one instantly whether a design is successful or unsuccessful. What *is* difficult is the correcting of an unsuccessful design. So break down the areas for critical decision into:

1. The individual shapes, are they good or not?
2. The total shape, is it good or not?
3. The shapes left *between* areas or motifs, are they good or not?
4. The colour or colours, are they pleasing?
5. The texture of the yarn and the texture of the knotting, are they pleasing?
6. The effect of a total repeating pattern (if there is one), is it cohesive?

One can always get a 'yes' or 'no' to each query. With the elements broken down like this, one is able to correct design faults detail by detail, and thus create a satisfactory whole.

Fig. 65
a Poor shapes: unpleasant lines and rings; the tatting pulled out of its natural formation; picots poorly placed.
b Satisfactory shapes: lines and rings forming good, natural curves; the tatting taking up its natural lines; picots placed and sized integrally to the design; interesting contrast of large and small rings.

69

If one still has difficulty with the design, pin it up and forget it totally. Maybe leave it as long as two or three days, then take it by surprise and the answer to your problem will often be apparent. Familiarity breeds not only contempt but also subjectivity! It is sometimes only possible to be objective about a piece of work by practically severing one's connections with it.

Using colour

To many people, particularly those with no design training, colour is a problem and therefore avoided. This is made easy by the large range of yarns available in varying shades of white and cream, and the fact that tatting looks very pleasing in these colours. Silver and gold yarns are also very easy to use as these invariably look well and one can achieve very satisfactory results with whites, creams, silver and black, or creams, golds and naturals. The problems arise when pure colour is contemplated. Two main factors should be borne in mind. Firstly, are the colours at one's disposal pleasing in themselves? Manufacturers' colour ranges vary greatly in their colour quality. If you are not satisfied with what you find, dye some yarns with natural dyes, better known as vegetable dyes (see Bibliography). The resulting colours are beautiful in the extreme. Secondly, remember that it takes painters much of their lives to handle colour, so be modest in your aims. A good beginning is to choose one colour and its neighbours in the spectrum and work in terms of shades and variations of these. The cope on page 89, for instance, was made in about ten variations of magenta and orange. Study paintings, not perhaps the whole painting but one section of it, and consider in detail how the colours have been used. What are the colours, what are their relationships to one another and in what amount has each colour been used? Use the pin-board and glass jars as repositories for coloured yarns and coloured matter in general so that colour, like graphic images, sinks into your consciousness and becomes an intrinsic part of your design vocabulary.

11 Completed objects, fabrics and design suggestions

The preceding chapters should have furnished the reader with a basic understanding of tatting construction sufficient to allow her to design and produce totally original work. On the following pages, there are illustrations in photographs and drawings of pieces of work which may spark off ideas, and information is given on how to produce them.

Fabric designs using simple motifs

In fig. 67, the designer has taken the simple ring, embellished with picots in varying sizes, produced in 'Novacord' (thread no. 15) and placed on different types of fabric in various ways. *a* is on net, *c* on felt and in *b*, the velvet is gathered over buttons to form puckering and would make excellent dress, smock or coat yokes and cuffs.

In fig. 68*a* and *b*, again the simple ring has been used. *a* is a blouse neck and the rings have been placed in a form to echo the feeling of the fabric to which they are attached. The rings were produced in pairs and then sewn together. In *b*, rings and beads are attached to chiffon and would make excellent blouse sleeves. *c* is hexagons of rings with exaggerated picots, which are then appliquéd to fabric. *d* is more complex, with lines as well as rings. It could be used for many purposes, some of which are illustrated in fig. 69:

a. Blind edging: the tatting is left without picots to give it a clean, direct look. The edge is embellished with small, wooden beads and the 'pull' is a metal ring or wooden ball. The background could be cut away or not, as desired.
b. The tatting is embellished with picots, which give a highly decorative effect. Again, the background could be cut away or not.

c. The blind is bound and embellished with tassels.
d. Pillow and sheet edging (and obviously many other like uses): the ground would not be cut away because of laundering.
e. The design is attached to the lamp-shade with a suitable adhesive.

General working instructions for the large motif are as follows:

With one shuttle:
Ring 11 dk, p, 2 dk, lp, 2 dk, p, 9 dk, cr.
*Leave ½ inch (13 mm.) length of thread.
Ring 6 dk, join to last p of previous r, 5 dk, p, 2 dk, lp, 2 dk, p, 9 dk, cr.
Rep from * 4 times.
Leave ½ inch (13 mm.) of thread.
Ring 6 dk, join to last p of previous r, 5 dk, p, 2 dk, lp, 2 dk, p, 6 dk, p, 3 dk, cr.
Leave ⅛ inch (3 mm.) length of thread.
Ring 1 dk, join to last p of previous r, 4 dk, 9 graded p, each separated by 2 dk, 4 dk, p, 1 dk, cr.
Leave ⅛ inch (3 mm.) length of thread and knot the thread around the base of the 7th r.
Ring 3 dk, join to last p of previous r, 6 dk, p, 2 dk, lp, 2 dk, p, 5 dk, p, 6 dk, cr.
*Leave ½ inch (13 mm.) thread and knot around base of the 6th r.
Ring 9 dk, join to last p of previous r, 2 dk, lp, 2 dk, p, 5 dk, p, 6 dk, cr.
Rep from * 5 times, leaving last p off last r.

The smaller motifs are worked in the same manner with fewer repeats. The rings have 7 p separated by 3 dk. The edging is a scroll.

Fig. 74 shows a random fabric and fig. 73 suggestions for its application. It was produced from simple, single rings, in varying sizes and colours, whites, ochres, silvers and golds. These were placed together to form a pleasing design and then sewn with 'invisible' thread. The fabric forms its own random edge.

In fig. 77 are asymmetrical pentagon shapes of rings with tails of long picots, produced by knotting on a second thread. Suggestions for their application are given in fig. 78.

In fig. 75, we see two more applications of the simple ring. The chains were worked in silver thread no. 11, the ends of each ring finished off. To make the rings interlink, the previous ring is slipped on to the loop of thread forming the new ring. The fabric was produced in silver thread no. 10, and uses the principle shown in fig. 27d. The size of the mesh and the decorative quality and size of the ring are capable of infinite variation so that the idea has many applications. It is very important always to get the length of unworked thread exactly the same length – this can be marked with a pin.

Other applications of the net-like fabric are shown in fig. 76.

The skirt (*a*) is produced in silver thread and caught at each intersection to a rich backing fabric, with pearls or stones sewn on at the intersections at the same time. It has a decorative edge and a heavy belt.

The snood (*d*) is in metal thread or chenille and beads, starting from the centre and finished off with fine elastic.

The day hold-alls (*e*) are in heavy cottons or jutes, with the top row of rings slipped on to the handles. The small bag in metallic threads and stones is finished off with a scroll, the handles are tatted in lines with very heavy metallic thread over thick cording.

The curtains or room dividers (*f*) have a decorative edge at the bottom. The top row of rings is slipped on to a bar.

The bikini-shapes and belts in fig. 70, and the further applications of the idea shown in fig. 71, are all derived from a very simple motif produced in heavy yarn as follows:

Thread no. 13
Ring 1   2 dk, (p, 4 dk) × 3, p, 2 dk, cr.
Ring 2   2 dk, join to 4th p of 1st r, 4 dk, (p, 4 dk) × 2, p, 2 dk, cr.
Ring 3   As 2nd and joined to it.
Ring 4   2 dk, join to 4th p of 3rd r, 4 dk, (p, 4 dk) × 2, join to 1st p of 1st r, 2 dk, cr, fasten off.

This motif is then continued, working over a paper pattern or an actual garment, modifying the shape of the motif at the edges of the pattern where necessary.

a.   The bikini top and pants must be lined and elastic attached at top and legs of pants and underneath the bra.
b.   The day or evening jacket can be of varying lengths. The yarn chosen, whether thick white cotton, double Twilley's 'double gold', thick coloured tapestry wools or mohair, *must* make a large, firm motif. Some of the motifs could have a pearl or bead at the centre. There is an edging of rings, unattached to each other except at the base. The garment is unlined.
c.   The day or evening skirt has a heavy, leather belt to complement it. It is made on the same principle as the jacket, but has a loose lining.

Fig. 66
Tatting used to embellish garments.

Fig. 67
Rings with asymmetrical large picots.
a 'Novacord' on net.
b 'Novacord' on velvet.
c 'Novacord' and beads on felt.
Carole Powell, Birmingham Polytechnic
Art & Design Centre.

c

a

b

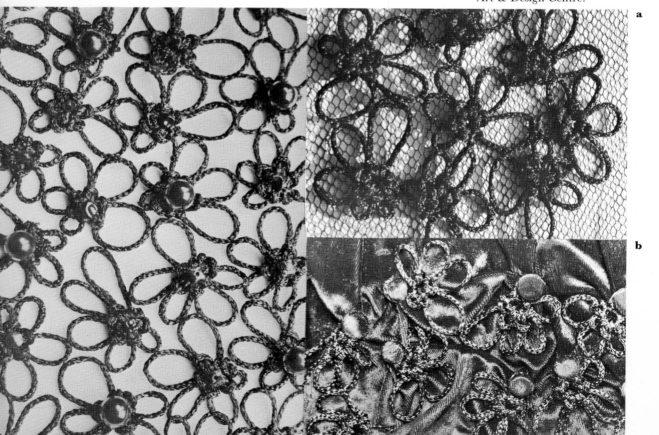

Fig. 68
a Blouse neck.
Gay Kettle, Birmingham Polytechnic
Art & Design Centre.
b Rings and beads on chiffon.
c Hexagons with large picots, appliquéd
to fabric.
d Edging design, suitable for varied
purposes.

Fig. 69
a and b Blind edgings.
c One motif only, used on a blind.
d As a pillow and sheet edging.
e On a lampshade.

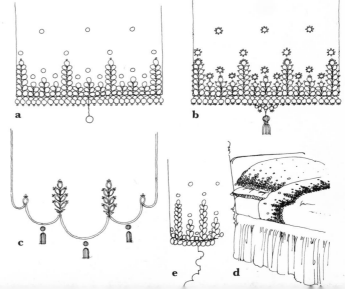

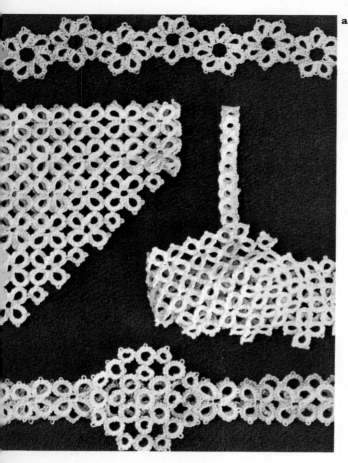

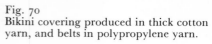

a Fig. 70
Bikini covering produced in thick cotton yarn, and belts in polypropylene yarn.

Fig. 71
Other design possibilities for the motif used in the bikini and belts (fig. 70).
b Jacket   c Skirt

Fig. 72
a Fashion application of lines.
b Tatting massed to form a rich, encrusted effect at the neck and yoke of a garment.
c Sleeve design (see fig. 68b).
d Headband (see fig. 82).
e and f Lampshade designs using lines.

Fig. 73
Other applications of the fabric in fig.
74
a Window blind with rings sewn on to
the fabric.
b Bodice.
c Lamp. Rings glued on to lamp and the
whole sprayed with clear lacquer or
fabric protector.

Fig. 74
Two aspects of a random fabric.

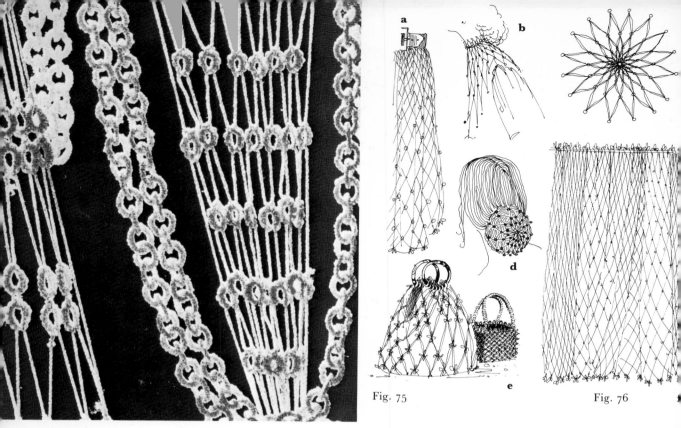

Fig. 75

Fig. 76

Fig. 77

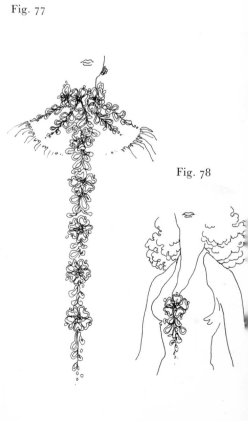

Fig. 78

Fig. 75
Rings and lengths of unworked thread to form net-like fabric. Interlinked rings to form chains.

Fig. 76
Applications of the net design.
a Evening or day skirt.
b Necklace or dress top, edged with a scroll.
c Circular formation.
d Snood.
e Day hold-alls and small bag.
f Curtains and room dividers.

Fig. 77
Asymmetrical pentagon shapes of rings with tails of long picots. Carole Powell, Birmingham Polytechnic Art & Design Centre (photographs, Geoffrey Waller).

Fig. 78
Applications of the motifs in fig. 77.

Jewelry

Fig. 81 shows a collection of very simple jewelry. The earrings were made as follows: *a* and *e* were made in gold metallic thread no. 16 by producing rings joined by picots or by producing isolated rings which were then sewn together. The cluster of beads at the base was necessary from a practical as well as an aesthetic point of view, as the weight was needed to make the earrings hang well.

b is in silver thread no. 10 – one ring with a picot on each side, one of which hooks on to the earring screw and one of which is joined to a second ring. To this second ring is attached an elongated scroll, which forms a bell shape, and lines of threaded beads come down on to the rings of the scroll to meet at a central point.

c uses the chain technique, illustrated in fig. 75.

f is composed of rings which have long picots. These long picots are threaded through the hole of a bead and then may be joined to another ring (see page 51).

The earrings (*d*), composed of a small, more complex motif, are made as follows:

In thread no. 16 (gold)
Ring 1 6 dk, p, 4 dk, (p, 2 dk) × 2, p, 4 dk, p, 6 dk, cr, tw.
Line 1 2 dk, p, 6 dk, tw.
Ring 2 4 dk, p, 5 dk, (p, 2 dk) × 2, p, 5 dk, p, 4 dk, cr, tw.
Line 2 6 dk, p, 6 dk, tw.
Ring 3 4 dk, join to 2nd r, 4 dk, (p, 2 dk) × 2, (p, 4 dk) × 2, cr, tw.
Line 3 5 dk, p, 5 dk, tw.
Ring 4 4 dk, join to 3rd r, 3 dk, (p, 2 dk) × 2, p, 3 dk, p, 4 dk, cr, tw.
Line 4 4 dk, p, 4 dk, tw.
Ring 5 3 dk, join to 4th r, 3 dk, (p, 2 dk) × 2, p, 6 dk, cr, tw.
Line 5 4 dk, p, 2 dk, tw.
Ring 6 (base) 6 dk, (p, 1 dk) × 2, p, 6 dk, cr, tw.
Line 6 2 dk, join to line 5, 4 dk, tw.
Ring 7 6 dk, (p, 2 dk) × 2, (p, 3 dk) × 2, cr, tw.
Line 7 4 dk, join to line 4, 4 dk, tw.
Ring 8 4 dk, join to 7th r, 3 dk, (p, 2 dk) × 2, p, 3 dk, p, 4 dk, cr, tw.
Line 8 5 dk, join to line 3, 5 dk, tw.
Ring 9 4 dk, join to 8th r, 4 dk, (p, 2 dk) × 2, (p, 4 dk) × 2, cr, tw.
Line 9 6 dk, join to line 2, 6 dk, tw.
Ring 10 4 dk, join to 9th r, 5 dk, (p, 2 dk) × 2, p, 5 dk, p, 4 dk, cr, tw.
Line 10 6 dk, join to line 1, 2 dk, tie end of line 10 to base of ring 1, and finish off.

Fig. 79
Necklace of clear glass 1 inch (25 mm.)
marbles, clear glass beads and gold
metallic thread.

Fig. 80 (above and opposite)
Necklaces in silver and gold, all designed
on the dressmakers' stand.

Fig. 79 shows a necklace of clear glass marbles (1 inch (25 mm.)
in diameter), smaller clear glass beads and gold metallic
thread no. 16. Two five-ring shapes of metallic thread were
made, joined together at the picots, and the marble slipped in
before the last picot was joined. The yarn-ends were then
passed through a glass bead and fastened off firmly on the
tatting surrounding the next marble. The end-ties are crochet.

In fig. 80 is a collection of necklaces, all designed on the
dressmaker's stand. *b* is composed of individual motifs, embellished with beads. Instructions for the motif are on page 79.
The necklace matches the earrings (*d*) illustrated in fig. 81*d*.
c is a necklace formed of rings with ribbon links.

Fig. 81
Earrings in gold, silver and glass.

Instructions for necklace *c* are as follows:
In thread no. 10 (silver)
Ring 1   4 dk, p, 4 dk, cr, fasten off.
Ring 2   2 dk, join to 1st r, 6 dk, p, 4 dk, cr, fasten off.
Ring 3   2 dk, join to 2nd r, 8 dk, p, 6 dk, cr, fasten off.
Ring 4   2 dk, join to 3rd r, 10 dk, p, 8 dk, cr, fasten off.
Ring 5   2 dk, join to 4th r, 12 dk, p, 10 dk, cr, fasten off.
Ring 6   2 dk, join to 5th r, 14 dk, p, 12 dk, cr, fasten off.
Ring 7   2 dk, join to 6th r, 16 dk, p, 14 dk, cr, fasten off.
Ring 8   2 dk, join to 7th r, 8 dk, p, 9 dk, (p, 1 dk) × 3, 8 dk, p, 6 dk, cr, fasten off.

Make as many motifs as required to go round neck, joining them together either with the picots on the eighth rings or with stitches or links of ribbon. This motif also makes excellent fringe-like edging for garments (hips and sleeves).

e is another necklace formed of rings, instructions for which are as follows:

In thread no. 10 (silver)
Ring 1   4 dk, p, 4 dk, cr, fasten off.
Ring 2   2 dk, join to 1st r, 8 dk, p, 6 dk, cr, fasten off.
Ring 3   2 dk, join to 2nd r, 12 dk, p, 10 dk, cr, fasten off.
Ring 4   2 dk, joined to 3rd r, 16 dk, p, 14 dk, cr, fasten off.
Ring 5   2 dk, join to 4th r, * 8 dk, p, 9 dk, (p, 1 dk) × 3, 8 dk, p, 6 dk, cr *, fasten off.
Ring 6   2 dk, join to centre top of 5th r, rep from * to * (ring 5).
Ring 7   As previous ring.
Make enough motifs to go around the neck, leaving $\frac{1}{4}$ inch (6 mm.) space between.

Joining the motifs:
Ring   1 dk, join to right side picot of 5th r of first motif, 4 dk, join to left side picot of 5th r of second motif.
3 dk, cr, fasten off.
Join all ring 5s together like this.
Likewise ring 6s and 7s.
Darn in all ends and attach fasteners.

d is a necklace formed in two parts. The neckband is a scroll. The fall is composed of isolated motifs held together with invisible nylon thread falling from a series of three-ring shapes around the neck. The two parts are joined together and the stones held in by means of crochet.

a is a necklace of rings and beads (see fig. 81*f*).

Fig. 82
Bracelet or cuff in silver elastic thread no. 18. Composed of two scrolls and embellished with stones.

Fig. 83
Gold metallic thread no. 16 and pearls on velvet ribbon, which could be either a choker or a belt.

a

b

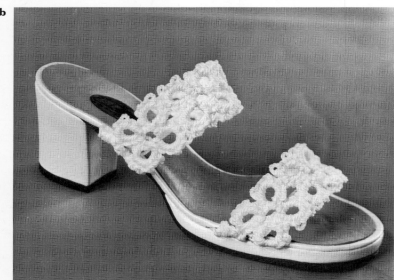

Fig. 84
a Day sandals. Tops designed and
produced by Judy Roberts. Sandal
bases supplied by Bally shoes, Norwich.
b Day sandal. Tops designed and
produced by Judy Roberts. Sandals
made up by Clarks of Street, Somerset.

Footwear

From jewelry we move on to decorative designs for footwear.
The sandal tops in fig. 84a were all worked in polypropylene
yarn (no. 19) which is immensely strong, and the motifs were
worked very tightly to eliminate all further movement of the
knots and any tendency to stretch out of shape. Rings and
shapes of rings were the basic motifs used, put together to
form shapes fitted over the foot.

Fig. 85
Evening sandals. Tops designed and
produced by Judy Roberts. Sandals
made up by Clarks. (The cloggs are
reinforced by a complete grosgrain
upper underneath the tatting.)

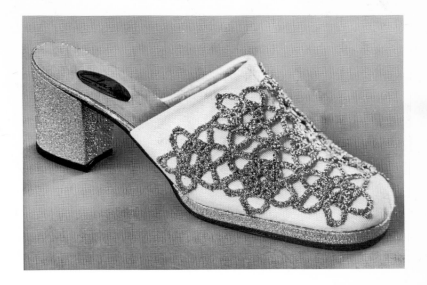

The biggest problem lies in securing the sandal top to the
base in a satisfactory manner. Sometimes sandal bases can be
bought with a canvas or rope edging to the sole to which the
upper can be sewn. Another solution is to procure wooden
sandal bases and nail the uppers on to them. A third solution
is to make the uppers with extra length. This is then turned
in, nailed to the horizontal of the sole, fortified with a very
strong adhesive and an 'inner-sole' placed over the work. It
should be mentioned that a number of small bespoke shoe-
makers still exist who could help you.

The sandal-tops in fig. 84*b* are made out of white nylon cord
as follows:

Ring   2 dk, p, * 3 dk, (p, 3 dk) × 3, p, 2 dk, cr *.
Ring   2 dk, join to 1st r, rep from * to *.
Work two more rings to form a square motif.
Work six motifs joined together for instep strap and five
motifs for toe strap. Carry thread across back of motifs instead
of working each one separately to give extra strength.

The evening slippers (fig. 85) were made with thread no. 22
(gold):
Ring   2 dk, p, 3 dk, lp, 3 dk, p, 2 dk, cr.
          * tw, line of 5 dk, p, 5 dk, tw.
Ring   2 dk, join to 1st r, 3 dk, join to lp of 1st r, 3 dk, p, 2 dk,
          close *.
Repeat from * to * 5 more times, finish off.
Join motifs in rows of two, three and four.

Fig. 86
Tatting used in conjunction with perspex ('plexiglass').

Abstract designs

We now move on to three purely abstract concepts. 'Jute Monster' (fig. 87) is a space-hanging composed of jute fibre and jute yarn, tatted. The tatting uses the line in its freest form and rings and shapes of rings form three-dimensional shapes. The hanging was finally stiffened with P.V.A. solution.

Tatting can be used to make further three-dimensional forms of a finer nature than 'Jute Monster' and in conjunction with a construction of perspex ('Plexiglass') can make airy, three-dimensional formations (fig. 86). Again the tatting was stiffened. The actual shapes were formed by making two circles composed of the scroll and joining these together to form shapes like cotton-reels.

Fig. 87
Jute Monster (detail).
2′6″ × 5′0″ × 9″ (76 × 152 × 23 cm.)

86

Fig. 88 shows how tatting can accentuate the design forms utilized in a decorative panel for the back of an antique-shop window. The panel was carried out in silver and gold fabric and threads, and tatting was the obvious choice for accentuating in a decorative way the curved lines of the design.

The puppet (fig. 89) resulted from college research into some aspect of historic ornament. The student chose Javanese shadow puppets as her subject and the piece is her answer to the part of the project in which she was instructed to 'select those aspects that you find most exciting and begin to express them in a more personal way. Organize in different ways the colour, line, shape or texture, whilst still retaining the essential elements of the original style.' The piece is worked mostly in lines.

Fig. 88
Two separate areas of a decorative panel for the background of an antique-shop window. (Property of Bambers Antiques, Kidderminster)

 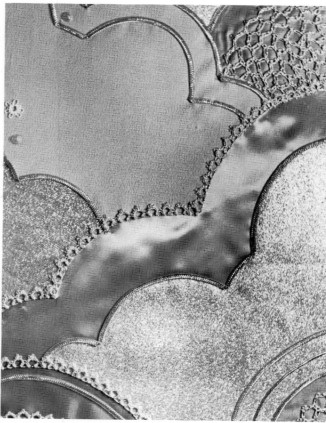

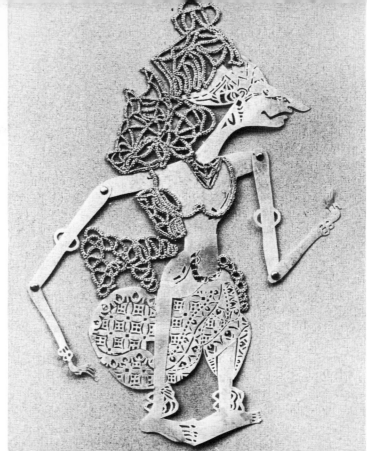

Fig. 89
A Javanese shadow puppet with
alternative decoration. Gay Kettle,
Birmingham Polytechnic Art &
Design Centre.

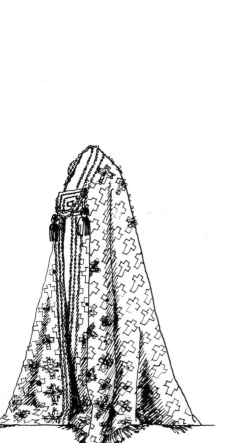

Fig. 90
A handwoven wool cope in magentas
and vermilions. (Property of the
Reverend Donald Watson, St Peters
Church, Kinver, Worcestershire)

A handwoven cope

Finally, we have tatting used to accent the richness and
texture of a cope (fig. 90). The cope was woven by hand in
magenta and vermilion wool with a pattern of crosses on a
ground. Elaboration was required as further textural interest
rather than dominating shapes, so wool rope, tatted motifs
and wool tassels embellished with tatting were produced in
the same general colours and yarns and high-lighted with
stones and sequins.

After the weaving was finished a tracing was made of the
woven cross motif, the desired design drawn on the tracing and
tatted accordingly (fig. 91).

Since the cope's colours were magenta and vermilion, the
required colour and lustre was impossible to find in tatting
and crochet yarns, so a composite three-fold yarn was created
of two strands of 2/12s vermilion mercerized weaving cotton,
and one strand of 477 denier magenta lurex gimp (Hutchinson's Shimmerette). Because the lurex gimp was slightly
rough, the tatting stitches were not pulled quite so tightly as
usual.

The cross is produced as follows:

With one shuttle, and leaving an 18 inch (46 cm.) end of yarn hanging

1. *Ring* 2 dk, (p, 4 dk) × 7, 2 dk (A). This fits around a paste jewel.
2. With the long end tensioned over the left hand and working with the shuttle thread, make a line of 12 double knots and pull into a curve (B).
3. *Ring* 6 dk, p, 4 dk, lp, 2 dk, lp, 4 dk, p, 6 dk (C).
4. Repeat 2 (D).
   Take both threads and knot around point E.
5. Pull a loop of the shuttle thread through picot (F) on ring A, slip shuttle through, pull tight.
6. *Ring* 10 dk.
7. Repeat 5 through next picot.
8. Repeat 3.
   Repeat 5, 6, 5, 3 twice.
9. Repeat 5 and 6.
10. End off by knotting or sewing.

The supporting smaller shapes were either shapes of eight rings or *f* in fig. 50.

The tassel covering was formed with two threads by first making a shape of seven rings, then a scroll, and joining the scroll to the shape by the picots at the heads of the seven rings. The form was then slipped over the tassel head (fig. 92).

Fig. 91

Fig. 92
Details of tassels on the cope (photograph Geoffrey Waller).

Fig. 93
Details of the body of the cope. Various simple shapes enclose stones and paillettes (photograph, Geoffrey Waller).

Bibliography

Books on tatting

Some of the older books are in the library of the Victoria and Albert Museum, London. Some books and most leaflets available from 'The Needlewoman Shop', 146 Regent Street, London W1R 6BA (by mail if necessary). Leaflets are obtainable from needlework shops. Books with historical information are starred.

Ashdown, E. A. *Tatting* Craft Notebook Series, USA 1961

Attenborough, Bessie *The Craft of Tatting* G. Bell & Son, London 1972

The Basic Book of Macramé and Tatting Octopus Books, London 1973

Caulfeild and Saward *Dictionary of Needlework* 1882

Crosier, Helen *Crochet and Tatting* G. Bell & Son, London 1953

Dillmont, Thérèse de *Tatting* D.M.C. Library, Editions Th. de Dillmont, Mulhouse, France

Dillmont, Thérèse de *Encyclopaedia of Needlework* Editions Th. de Dillmont, Mulhouse, France

*Groves, Sylvia *History of Needlework Tools and Accessories* David & Charles, Newton Abbot and Arco Publishing, New York 1973

Hoare, Lady Katherine *The Art of Tatting* Longmans, London 1910

*Nicholls, Elgiva *Tatting* Vista Books, London 1962 and Taplinger Publishing Co., New York 1965

Nicholls, Elgiva *A New Look in Tatting* Tiranti Ltd, London 1959

Orr, Anne *Anne Orr's Crochet Books Nos. 13 and 35* Nashville, Tennessee 1935

Riego de la Branchardière, Eleanore *Tatting Edgings and Insertions* London 1866

Pattern leaflets with tatting instructions
Time for Tatting   Coats Sewing Group Book 813
Learn Tatting   Coats Sewing Group Book 1088

Pattern leaflets giving patterns only
Coats leaflets 768, 919, 994, 1072, 1127 (UK)
Coats & Clarks booklet 208 (USA)

Miscellaneous reading

Dyeing
Lesch, Alma   *Vegetable Dyeing*   Watson-Guptill, New York
    1970
Thurstan, Violetta   *The Use of Vegetable Dyes*   Dryad Press,
    Leicester 1967

General
Hartung, Rolf   *Creative Textile Craft*   Batsford, London and
    Van Nostrand Rheinhold, New York 1964

Design sources
Brodatz, Phil   *Textures: a Photographic Album for Artists and
    Designers*   Dover Publications, New York 1966
Feininger, Andreas   *Forms in Nature and Life*   Thames &
    Hudson, London and Viking Press, New York 1966
Strache, Wolf   *Forms and Patterns in Nature*   Pantheon Books,
    New York 1973

General craft magazines
Craft Horizons   Magazine of the American Craftsman's Coun-
    cil, 29 West 53rd Street, New York
Crafts   Crafts Advisory Committee, 28 Haymarket, London

Suppliers

Shuttles

Retail supply
'The Needlewoman Shop', 146 Regent Street, London W1R
6BA (goods can be ordered by mail)
Most needlework shops

Makers
C. J. Bates & Son Inc., Chester, Connecticut
The Boye Needle Company, 4343 N. Ravenswood Avenue,
Chicago, Illinois
Henry Milward & Sons Ltd: shuttles distributed through J. &
P. Coats, 155 St Vincent Street, Glasgow
Abel Morrell Ltd, Clive Works, Redditch, Worcestershire

Threads

Retail supply
'The Needlewoman Shop', 146 Regent Street, London W1R
6BA (threads can be ordered by mail)
Most needlework shops

Makers
J. & P. Coats Ltd, 155 St Vincent Street, Glasgow (mercer
crochet available in most countries except USA)
H. G. Twilley Ltd, Stamford, Lincolnshire (threads can be
ordered from 'The Needlewoman Shop'; not available in
USA)
Coats & Clark Inc., 430 Park Avenue, New York

Sundries

'Celotex' soft board: obtainable from hardware stores

Pilkingtons' (UK) diffused reflection glass: obtainable through the glass merchant

P.V.A. and 'Hyplar': obtainable from artists' suppliers

'Scotchgard' fabric protector: obtainable from the 'notions' or sundries counter at big department stores

Window blinds: kits for making your own available from Bedford Products Ltd, 289 High Street, Watford, Herts.

Index

Abbreviations 8, 37
Abstract designs 86, 87
Adhesives 30, 53
Artists 15
Attaching
    (tatting to another element) 55
    (via the picot) 55
Authors 12, 13, 14, 15

Bags 78
Back (of the work) 33
Ball-thread 41, 42
Bars 18
Basic shapes 20, 24, 25, 32, 33, 34,
    37, 69, 86, 87
Beads 51, 64, 65, 79, 80, 81
Beeton 13
Belts 73, 76
Bikini 73, 76
Blinds 71, 72, 75, 77, 94
Blocking 53
Blocking-pad 26, 54, 55
Blouse 65, 75, 77
Books 12, 13, 14, 15, 91
Bracelet 31, 82
Buttonhole stitch 55, 56

Camera 59, 63
Caulfeild & Saward 13
Celotex 26, 54, 94
Chains 18, 72, 78, 79
Clover 25
Colour 50, 70
Cotton 9, 51
Cope 70, 89, 90
Cow-hitch knot 17
Crochet 51
Curtains 73, 78

Daisy 25, 37
Design 59, 64
Designing 59, 63, 64, 65, 67, 68, 69,
    70
Design sources 59, 60, 61, 62, 63
Dillmont, Therese de 13, 14, 31
Double knot 17, 22, 23, 29, 30
Double stitch 17
Drawing 59, 60
Drawing implements 59
Dressmaker's stand 26
Dyeing 70

Earrings 31, 79, 82
Edgings 35
Ends (fastening off) 30, 53

Fabric (tatted) 36
Fabrics 51, 55
Face (of the work) 33
Felt 55
Feston 18
Festoon 18
Fine-Art Concepts 59
Finishing Processes 53, 54
Frames 56, 57

Glass 57, 94

Half-ring 24, 38, 39
Heath-Robinson, W. 60
History 11
Hoare, Lady 13, 14
Hooks 27
Hyplar 56, 94

Independent thread 23
Insertion (of tatting) 55

Ironing 54
'Invisible' sewing thread 56

Jackets 73, 76
Jewellery 31, 56, 79, 82, 83
Josephine ring 24, 31
Juxtaposing 67

Knotting 11

Lace 17
Lark's head knot 17
Laundering 54
Leather 55
Light fittings 72, 75, 76, 77
Lines 18, 23, 43, 45, 47, 48, 49, 76,
    88, 89
Locking stitch 24
Lozenge 23

Macramé 51
Marie, Queen of Romania 13
Magazines 92
Medallions 25
Mignonette stitch 25, 40, 72, 73, 78
Mock-rings 24, 46
Mock-up 64, 65
Morawska, Alice 14
Mounts 56, 57
Mounting work 56, 57

Natural shapes 23, 24, 25
Necklace 31, 80, 81, 83
Net-like fabric 78
Nicholls, Elgiva 14, 15
Node stitch 24, 46
Notebook (tatting) 26, 68

Objects 71
Oillet 38, 39

Paintings 15
Patterns 27
Pattern leaflets 92
Pearl 18
Pearl loop 18
Perspex (plexiglass) 57
Photography 59, 61, 62, 63
Picots 18, 20, 23, 31, 32, 33, 44, 74,
    75, 78
Pillow 72, 75
Pins 54
Pinboard 26, 54
Pinning 54
Planning 67

Portraits 15
Protection (fabric) 54, 56, 57
Puppet 88, 89
Purl 18
P.V.A. 56, 94

Random fabrics 72, 77
Rapidographs 59
Ribbon 34
Riego de la Branchardière 12, 13,
    14
Rings 17, 18, 23, 30, 31, 32, 37, 64,
    65, 71, 74, 75
Room dividers 73
Rosette 12
Rounds 24
Running-line 23

Sampling 50
Scallop 25
Scroll 25, 64
Scotchgard fabric protector 54, 94
Sculptural qualities 87
Shaping 68
Shoes 84, 85
Shuttles 11, 12, 26, 27, 28, 41, 42
Skirt 73, 74, 76, 78
Straight thread 18
Strips of tatting 34, 36, 74, 75
Suede 55

Tassels 90
Tatting characteristics 17, 18, 20,
    22, 23
Tatting names 16, 17
Tatting terms 23, 24, 25
Tatting tools 26, 27, 28
Tatting technique 29, 42
Tension 42
Threads 9, 27, 50, 52
Traditional formations 24, 25

Unturned knot 24, 33, 42
Unworked thread 24, 39, 40, 52

V. & A. museum 15
Variations of approach 50

Wallhangings 31
Weaving 21
Winding of shuttles 29
Wheel 25, 37

Yarns 9